MW01061279

FIRST
HIRED
LAST FIRED

How to Become Irreplaceable
in Any Job Market

ANITA AGERS-BROOKS

LEAFWOOD
PUBLISHERS

FIRST HIRED, LAST FIRED
How to Become Irreplaceable in Any Job Market

Copyright 2013 by Anita Agers-Brooks

ISBN 978-0-89112-320-0

Printed in the United States of America

ALL RIGHTS RESERVED
No part of this publication may be reproduced, stored in a retrieval system, or trans-mitted in any form by any means—electronic, mechanical, photocopying, or other-wise—without prior written consent.

All scripture quotations, unless otherwise indicated, are taken from the Holy Bible, New International Version®, NIV®. Copyright ©1973, 1978, 1984, 2011 by Biblica, Inc.™ Used by permission of Zondervan. All rights reserved worldwide. www.zondervan.com The "NIV" and "New International Version" are trademarks registered in the United States Patent and Trademark Office by Biblica, Inc.™

The Author is represented by and this book is published in association with the literary agency of WordServe Literary Group, Ltd., www.wordserveliterary.com.

Cover design by Marc Whitaker
Interior text design by Sandy Armstrong

Leafwood Publishers is an imprint of
Abilene Christian University Press
1626 Campus Court
Abilene, Texas 79601

1-877-816-4455
www.leafwoodpublishers.com

13 14 15 16 17 18 / 7 6 5 4 3 2 1

Table of Contents

Acknowledgments

No book would be complete without a long list of thanks from the author. Mine is no different. I humbly ask forgiveness in advance if I forget to include your name, for many have been irreplaceable in making this project possible.

First behind God is my husband, Ricky. In more than thirty years together, you've surprised and delighted me most during this journey. Your willingness to take an extra role in caring for me, our home, our children, and our grandchildren is the main reason this book exists. My love and appreciation extend beyond my ability to communicate. So I'll say it simply, thank you.

To my parents, who raised me with a good work ethic, I appreciate your discipline, even though I didn't think I would. And to my siblings, who were the unhappy recipients of my many failures as a leader. Thank you for forgiveness, prayer, and support. I truly love you all.

To my best girlfriend, Mary. We've lost count of our years of friendship, but, whatever the span, I'm grateful for your encouragement, for your wisdom, and that you sharpen me like iron. You make me a better person.

To Val, for without you, I couldn't have learned to write. Your support provided the time I needed to dig in and seriously do what my heart desired.

To Karen Porter, who mentored me and shaped me into a much better writer than I was and encouraged me to become better than I am. You can't know how much I appreciate your investment in my raw talents.

To CLASS, Christian Leaders, Authors, and Speakers Seminars. God used you first, to set me on the course he planned before I was born. Because of your hard work, writers like me have a place to learn and grow.

To Karen, Sharon, Laura, Ashley, Carol, Kathy, Tera, Betty Ann, Kent, Sherry, Rusty, Art, Jan, Tom, Judy, Wes, Jenny, Kevin, Mike, Georgia, and many other Prayer Warriors, I am eternally grateful. And to Darla, who saw the vision of my name on a cover before I did. Thank you for giving to the Lord. You helped me honor him.

To Barbara Scott, my original agent with WordServe Literary, along with Greg, Alice, and the rest of the team. I thank you so much for taking a risk. I pray I can give back to you. And to my fellow WordServe authors, what a support you are; I praise God for each and every one of you.

To the team at Leafwood Press, thank you for transforming this into a book worth reading. Your diligence exemplifies good work.

To the crew at Ozark Outdoors Riverfront Resort. No wonder people come from all over the world—you guys make it beautiful. Thank you for the testing, the proving, and the experience that provided so much fodder for the principles in this book. The feast-and-famine element of resort work certainly forces you to do more with less. The results in our Missouri Eden are spectacular.

I must say thanks to the professional organizations and businesses who provided insights, educational opportunities, and a place to share much of what I've learned: Professional Paddlesports Association, the National RV & Campground Association, the Missouri RV & Campground Association, CLASS, Stonecroft International Ministries, Christian Writer's Guild, and many clients who allow me to share the vision for people who can make a difference in the everyday, placed exactly where they are.

I must especially point to the current members of The Power Circle, a group of business owners from different parts of America. I appreciate the distinct privilege of facilitating your quest for growth in the face of challenging conditions. Thank you, Mike, of Voyageur Canoe Outfitters, Josh, of Mohican Adventures, Jack, of Adventures Unlimited, Bear, of Ozark Outdoors Riverfront Resort, and Lee, of River and Trail Outfitters. Our explorations have further enhanced the findings in this book. For those who participated previously, thank you as well.

To all my Facebook friends, Twitter followers, LinkedIn connections, and Pinterest followers, thank you for encouragement, research opportunities, and input.

For every employer I've ever had, thank you for failures and successes. Without practical application, this book would be theory, rather than something tried and true. In particular, I want to express my appreciation to Jim Barnett, who saw a spark in a twenty-something woman, and taught her how to take the raw talent and work it into something more valuable.

And finally, to God who mixed my DNA, along with those who contributed physically to the process. You made me who I am, equipped with the desire to write, the willingness to learn, and the compulsion to share.

Preface

Scan any reputable publication and the message reads the same. We are in economic trouble on a global scale. Reports of debt crisis and slow trade around the world keep financial leaders guessing on what to do next. But what if you could help?

There's no question we are living in volatile times. Unprecedented unemployment rates, foreclosures, and business closings have caused pervasive anxiety. Bankruptcy isn't the easy option of the past. Governments are near collapse and crying out for intervention.

To make matters worse, college tuition and student debt are at all-time highs, while the percentage of available jobs is at an all-time low. Our future isn't as bright as it used to be.

So how can you, an everyday person, looking for work or in an everyday job, with or without a degree or fancy resume, effect change? What if I told you it was possible? Whether you work in fast food or head up a Fortune 100, you can cause a positive domino effect that touches the world around you and, very possibly, beyond.

In the process, I believe you can position yourself to become irreplaceable. By applying the simple secrets in this book, you will prime yourself to stand out in an interview and, as an employee or company, to succeed for the long haul.

To do so, you don't need complicated formulaic equations, a pedigree education, or a huge investment of your money, or even time.

The qualifications are simple: humility, a teachable attitude, and the willingness to do something with what you learn. Then prepare yourself for the results.

I wrote this book because I want readers to experience the benefit of a secret I, and others, have discovered. The secret to getting a job and growing with it in positive ways. The secret to rising above the crowd and effecting real change. The secret to making a difference while you have breath in your body. A secret available to almost anyone, and one that's been tested successfully for thousands of years. An ancient text carries the key to simple mysteries in its tissuey pages. Ones that can benefit you and those you love for a greater good. Who doesn't want to leave an irreplaceable legacy when they depart this earth?

Crack open this ancient book and be prepared to gasp at what you find. Set your mind to discovering answers to help you at work or to get a job. Resolve to try specific principles found in the Bible for three months. If nothing changes, are you any worse off?

Four years ago, I set out on a quest to find out why some people weren't hired, why some were laid off, and why so many businesses were closing. After more than one hundred interviews, a definite pattern emerged. My next question: Is there anything we can do?

And then I realized my own experiences were littered with dos and don'ts. Though I've made mistakes, and continue to do so at times, there is no question the Bible, not a specialized degree, is the secret to my success.

I've followed specific steps taken by those who made a mark on history. They changed the world for themselves and others. They were irreplaceable people. I can't imagine anyone taking their place or doing what they did.

With that basis, I spoke with others. Many in today's culture know this same secret and use it for their own benefit. While the majority frets and worries about what tomorrow will bring, these savvy folks rest in the sure knowledge that time-tested biblical application saves lives and livelihoods. It doesn't guarantee freedom from problems, but then again, if we had no problems, we could have no miracles.

Each chapter includes a before and after story. The opening scenarios are fictionalized accounts based on truth, compilations of people I've interacted with, observed, or been told about. Because of a volume in patterns and in order to protect those involved, I created an account to represent the general theme. Equally, each after story is one part true example and one part my imagination. Some outcomes may seem dramatic, but, I assure you, similar reports occur daily. Read the newspaper or watch the news, lounge in a coffee shop or sit in a church pew, and you'll see what I mean.

PART ONE

Basic Principles

Chapter 1

The Joseph Factor

In order to be irreplaceable,
a difference must be evident.

"Anyone can be replaced." Often quoted, but is this an irrefutable truth? Or can someone become so valuable at work it's hard to imagine anyone else doing the job? I asked these questions in a two-year investigation to find out why some employees are favored and why others are easily discarded.

As part of my search, I considered my own experience as a leader. I've encountered a few rare employees who demonstrated integrity to such a degree that they became irreplaceable to me as a supervisor. I've fought to keep these people in my workforce, and, when they left, things weren't the same. Whether they knew it or not, these savvy folks set themselves apart by following centuries-old patterns.

There are formulas for success proven through millennia of practice. Irreplaceable employees dare to be different in a systematic way.

My examination of facts took me deep into the heart of the Bible. Whether you believe in this ancient text or not, it's hard to argue against its time-proven wisdoms. In my research, I discovered more than eight hundred passages related to work or labor. I believe if we studied and applied them today, a powerful and united workforce could result.

Where debt buries us, untold riches await our unearthing. Instead of giving jobs away, nations would rise to a place of leadership in the world's commerce. Pride would fall prey to humility rooted in a commitment of integrity. But it starts with the individual.

Let's face it, many people believe they work smarter, harder, and better than their peers. But do their ethics, their productivity, and their attitudes support this belief? In today's cynical world, can individuals still impact their job, family, community, nation, and the globe for a greater good? Can you become irreplaceable?

I've seen the difference when people work God's way and when they don't. You get what you give.

Gary's story is a prime example. For this book, I interviewed more than one hundred employees in various fields. The following fictionalized account portrays a compilation of a sad reality played out in businesses around the world. Let's peek inside the mind of a man who believes he's underappreciated and justifies his weak behavior.

The powerful scent of imitation leather and sandalwood caused Gary to sneeze. First Capital Mortgage Company's board members were meeting tomorrow, which meant someone overdid the commercial air fresheners. Gary didn't need cologne today. His clothes would smell of the earthy concoction by lunch.

He tried to smooth his rumpled shirt while he clocked in. The sound of male laughter caught his ear, so Gary made his way to the small group of huddled co-workers. He circled the group with a few friendly back-slapping and how-are-you greetings. Each man rewarded him with a varying degree of smile.

"Hey, are you putting money in the football pool or not? Everyone else is in, and the big game's tonight," Tom said.

"Yeah, I'll stop by your desk before I leave today, I promise," Gary said.

"As usual, a man of many words. I'll believe it when I see it."

Gary's hazel eyes sparkled and he cocked his right eyebrow. "Hey, I keep my promises."

Tom opened his mouth to respond but shut it just as quickly. Their chief financial officer, Mark, stormed up the hall wearing a focused frown. The huddled mass broke, and most of the men scurried to their posts, hoping Mark wouldn't note the inactivity. Gary wasn't fast enough and stood frozen in position, waiting for the assault.

When Mark caught you doing anything but work, punishment followed. It might not be formal, and Mark might not address the situation directly, but his reactions said you were on his blacklist.

Sensing danger, Gary offered Mark a verbal to do list.

Red-faced, Mark said, "Don't tell me what you're going to do, just do it. I've been waiting on that report for three days now, and it had better be on my desk by 3 P.M. No excuses this time." He barely broke stride as he marched off to find his next victim.

After Mark left, Gary shrugged his shoulders. He muttered while he walked, "If Mark would just listen and treat me like a human being, I might be able to finish that report. Every time I try to tell him my plans, he gets annoyed. He should appreciate me. I try a lot harder than some of the people who work here. He doesn't have to be such a jerk. If I were running this company, I'd listen to people."

For months, Gary had tried. Small talk about the family, flattering comments, and even gifts hadn't worked with Mark. Every attempt met a terse, "Don't you have work to do?"

"No matter what I say, he just doesn't like me." Disappointed but determined not to give up, Gary stopped muttering and whistled as he headed to his desk.

Once there, he grabbed his coffee cup and fell in step with Christy. They chatted briefly on the way to and from the office lounge. Fifteen minutes later, Christy headed to her own desk as Gary sat down to work. His mind wandered while he popped his earbuds in. He scrolled to the new album he'd downloaded last night. He needed to focus; Mark would have his head if he missed another deadline.

Gary started his daily routine. He checked e-mail, updated his Facebook status, checked the activities of his friends, and tweeted. Then he added charges to the expense voucher from his recent business trip, before preparing to get into the report Mark needed.

Gary typed two sentences when his iPhone vibrated. His wife, Denise, said, "Hi, honey, I just spoke with the plumber and he'll be at the house tomorrow. Can you take off?"

"I'm not sure. Mark's really on me today. Can't you do it?"

Denise sighed, "I'll see, but if I'm gone tomorrow, I can't leave in time to pick Emma up from practice tonight. Can you get her at five?"

"Yeah, I'm sure I can sneak out a few minutes early. Do you want me to get something for supper?"

A heavy breath signaled Denise's relief. "That would be great. Oh, I've gotta go, here comes my manager. Love you." The line went dead.

Gary put his phone back in his shirt pocket, clicked on Mark's report, and then stopped. He realized he needed to check his bank balance. He pulled up the online information and got his checkbook out. He hoped there was enough to pay the plumber. A few minutes later, an assistant manager walked by, so Gary clicked on the overdue report until the coast was clear. He pulled his account back up and after a quick reconciliation was relieved to find there was enough money for the house repairs.

He looked at his watch and gasped. It was almost time for lunch, and he hadn't even started that report. Beating back a twinge of guilt, Gary pushed hard for the next hour and twenty minutes. He even worked ten minutes into lunch to make up for the time he'd wasted in the morning.

The afternoon passed uneventfully. Gary finally put the last touches on his report just before two thirty. He sent a text to share the good news with his wife, and breathed deep with satisfaction. He wondered aloud, "Why do I put things off? It's not so bad once I get started."

Gary smiled sheepishly as Tonya walked by his cubicle and gave him a puzzled look. His outspoken musing must have been louder than he thought.

He celebrated the report completion by walking across the office to see Tom. They bantered about the upcoming play-offs. Tom challenged Gary with, "Put your money where your mouth is, buddy, and give me five bucks for the pool."

Gary chuckled as he dug the money out of his wallet. They were still laughing when Mark walked up behind Gary. The cloud on his face promised bad news.

"Th-tha-a-at report's on m-my desk and ready to go."

"Grab it and bring it to my office. I need to talk to you."

Gary felt queasy as he walked the hall toward Mark's office. He knocked on the door and entered at Mark's terse invitation. As Gary sat down, he saw Connie, the human resource manager. Gary flinched when Mark shut the door behind them.

"Gary, we have to make cuts. There's no way around it. The banking industry is suffering along with the rest of the nation in this recession. Positions must be eliminated, and yours is the first to go. Connie will help you clean out your desk. The necessary paperwork is done. You will get two weeks of severance pay, and we certainly wish you the best of luck. I'm sorry." Mark's tone of voice wasn't as soft as his final words.

With that Gary was dismissed, shocked into speechlessness. The report lay untouched on Mark's desk.

Connie escorted Gary to his desk. He numbly filled a box with all his personal items. When he was done, he took a last look at a piece of furniture he no longer recognized. Now empty of possessions and personality, it looked as bare as his soul felt.

Security came and walked beside Gary as he shuffled out the employee entrance for the last time. Head down, tears dangerously close to spilling, he noticed the door that had become invisible to him. Not since his early days of employment had his enthusiasm prompted him to push hard and prove himself. As his comfort in the company grew, his ambition waned. Soon, his routine mirrored that of fellow employees.

Now, however, he realized he would never cross this threshold again. Like many other people, he joined the ranks of the unemployed. Nausea punched him in the stomach as he stepped into the sunlight, and Gary wondered how any of this happened.

———

Whether your job is hidden behind the scenes or you stand in front of the public, saying, "May I help you?" meaningful work makes life worth living. Some are tasked with juggling the people and work processes as a manager, knowing full well they won't please everyone. Some try to keep up with ever-changing demands of bosses, who can't seem to make up their minds.

Many employees simply don't realize they have the power of choice in determining their outcomes. Without realizing it, they often give their own jobs away. It's as if an invisible thief sneaks around the corner and picks their pockets, plucking all but the lint. They never see it coming.

Most workers don't consider lost time theft. However, there is no difference between stealing time and stealing cash. Managers often meet people who wouldn't steal twenty dollars from their employer but take hundreds in time wasted.

Often, employees avoid personal responsibility by casting blame on each other. Factories, offices, construction sites, restaurants, service industries, and more are susceptible to attack. When employees engage in personal e-mails, Internet play, text messages, phone calls, inappropriate personal conversations, or other non-work-related activity, the risk is significant. Consider the following equation as an example:

- 2 employees paid $10 per hour × 6 inappropriate 15-minute distractions = $30 the thief has stolen
- 3 hours per day × 5 days = $150 per week stolen
- 3 hours per day × 20 work days = $600 stolen monthly
- Multiply $30 by 260 work days per year and the annual cost = $7,800

But the employer is not the only one to suffer. As procrastination rises and motivation decreases, individual employees lose inner satisfaction and peace. Employee raises, benefits, and sometimes the job itself are forfeited when a business struggles to make ends meet. The bottom line: everyone suffers.

I've employed people with college degrees whose behavior made them an employee I could do without. By the same token, I've hired folks with no credentials but who were teachable and acted on their desire to do more. It isn't a matter of intelligence—people can learn—it's a matter of what you do with what you learn. The difference is simple: study God's word and do something positive with the information inside.

In the book of Genesis, a man named Joseph put his heart into his work. His actions caused him to receive favor. He treated other people's property like his own. He worked as if he owned the business. If today's employees invested like Joseph, I believe the world we live in might look different. The change could start with you.

You have more power than you think. With intent, you can influence the world around you for your own benefit, but also for the benefit of others.

In its simplest form, integrity is doing the same thing whether you think someone can see you or not. At a deeper level, the power of extraordinary integrity shocks others to pay closer attention. Try it.

The next time you're sitting with other employees and gossip ensues, especially if you take part in any way, go back and apologize for your participation. Even if you simply listened but didn't speak.

Listening alone gives the impression that you condone the words of complaint and backstabbing.

Later, when you walk up and say, "I need to apologize," most people will automatically ask, "What for?" This is your opportunity to say something like this, "I shouldn't have talked about Nancy behind her back. I'm sorry. I was wrong." Leave it at that—period.

Excuses, blame, or qualifiers, like the word *but*, can negate anything else you say. It also shifts blame to someone else. For example, "I shouldn't have talked about Nancy behind her back, but when I heard all of you, it slipped out."

You must confess in purity and honesty with genuine remorse for this to work. Don't say anything about others—stick to what *you* did.

Take courage and become a hero in the workplace. The world needs more heroes. Since many of us spend more time with people at work than we do with our own families, what greater place to witness by our actions the life of Jesus Christ? Can you imagine him gossiping?

Don't worry about what others think, whether they laugh at you, or even turn on you. What's the worst thing someone might say behind your back? "I don't really like her, but I have to admit, she gets the job done."

Or do you prefer, "I thought he was supposed to be a Christian, but he spends more time talking than working"? The results depend on the pattern of your work habits. The choice is yours.

The model of Joseph shows us a secret to success in the workplace. Applying his wisdom can make you different. Joseph stands out as a man who not only impacted his immediate surroundings, but, because of his consistency, he saved individuals, families, commerce, and nations from destruction. His life made a huge difference. I can't imagine anyone else doing what Joseph did. He was irreplaceable. Several factors point to the reason why.

- Joseph believed in his God-given dreams. Though he was hated and others were jealous, he accepted his circumstances. Even when he was mocked and his brothers plotted to destroy him, Joseph submitted while he waited for his dreams to become reality (Gen. 37:5–20).

- Joseph endured torment at the hands of those with evil intent. He required mercy so he could be rescued from the clutches of disaster (Gen. 37:21–22).
- Joseph knew his limitations and went willingly when his brothers sold him out for their own personal gain (Gen. 37:26–28).
- Joseph needed blind faith. He didn't realize a rescue attempt was made after he was gone (Gen. 37:29).
- Joseph's dreams took him to foreign places, and he was put in relationship with strange people. Because he believed God and followed with his whole heart, Joseph was favored by the Lord. God blessed those Joseph served, and he influenced many others (Gen. 39:1–5).
- Joseph proved himself trustworthy by his common patterns of integrity. He conducted himself the same way whether anyone else could see or not. Even when there was an appearance of impropriety, Joseph did not make excuses or blame others. He waited in the darkest place for God's favor to shine (Gen. 39:6–23).
- Joseph helped those in need. He cared enough to ask why they were sad and interpreted their God-given dreams for them. Then he clearly communicated the request on his own heart (Gen. 40:1–15).
- Joseph spoke the truth, even when it wasn't what the other person wanted to hear. Even though it must have been painful (Gen. 40:16–22).
- Joseph held on when hope seemed to be lost to the selfishness of others. Over the passing of years, he fulfilled

his duties and took care of everyday business (Gen. 40:23, 41:1–8).

- Joseph was ready for the task when he was finally called back to service. Prepared by practice and pattern, he did not, however, take credit when it wasn't his due (Gen. 41:40).
- Joseph didn't slouch, play, or waste time when times were easy. Instead, like the ant, he took advantage of the opportunity. He worked hard and saved from the bounty. He prospered both professionally and personally because he was a wise steward over the blessings he and his master received. He trained others to do the same (Gen. 41:41–54).
- Joseph didn't hoard his abundance. He shared with those in need. Even those who had hurt him in the past. He remembered his dreams and trusted that the hardship was part of the plan to make him better (Gen. 41:55–57; 42:1–6).
- As a man of integrity, Joseph wasn't afraid to be bold in making his point. He demonstrated his authority and showed strength as the man in charge (Gen. 42:7–38; 43; 44).
- Joseph showered mercy on those who mistreated him, and the truth finally came out. He accepted the larger plan at work and blessed those who had cursed him. He shared his wealth with his former enemies (Gen. 45).
- Joseph didn't steal from his employer. He turned everything he collected over to the one who owned it. Joseph was content with what he had been given. He didn't resent not having more (Gen. 47:13–26).

If it hadn't been for Joseph's practice of integrity, many would have suffered and died.

Every company you work for, or with, affords you the honor of being a Joseph to them. Ask God to bless the work of your hands and that the overflow of those blessings would spill onto those around you. Treat the business as if you owned it.

Ask that your company would affect the county, state, federal, and global governments in positive ways. And keep your eyes open for opportunities to take action in accordance with the examples of those who obeyed God's formula for successful living.

I wonder how Gary's life might look had he chosen to practice integrity like Joseph.

—⁓—

Music filtered into Gary's fuzzy mind. Praise music, energetic and uplifting. He twisted onto his side, tempted to hit the snooze, until the aroma of Maxwell House Breakfast Blend rousted him from the last vestige of sleep. He palmed the off button on the clock, leaned over, kissed his wife lightly, and got up. He scuffed to the kitchen.

"Thank goodness for automatic timers," Gary said to himself while he poured a steaming cup of dark brew and settled at the table with his Bible. He bowed his head and prayed for wisdom, then dug into his study of Joseph.

A page of notes, two cups of coffee, and thirty minutes later, Gary closed his Bible and put everything away. He headed to the bedroom to wake his wife and get ready for work.

Gary listened to a message on the radio as he drove to the office. The speaker hit many of the same points he'd found in his personal study earlier. He chuckled and shook his head. "I hear you. Thanks for setting me straight."

When he walked inside the building whistling, John, one of his co-workers, said, "What are you so happy about?"

"I'm just rejoicing in this day the Lord has made," Gary said.

"You're nuts, you know that? Didn't you hear about Mike? He's the fourth one in two days they've let go. Who knows, we might be next."

"I heard, but I'm not going to let it keep me from doing my job. This is where my faith meets the road. I trust God more than my fears."

"Like I said, you're nuts." John shook his head and skulked down the hall.

Gary clocked in and walked toward the growing pitch of men's laughter. As he approached, Tom said, "Hey, buddy, do you want in on the football pool?"

"I appreciate it, but no thanks. I'd better stick with earning my money."

"Is a measly five bucks going to break you?" Tom elbowed the guy standing next to him.

Gary chuckled, "It isn't that. My convictions simply won't let me waste it. Five dollars could go into my children's college fund, or even better, it could help feed someone who's starving. I appreciate the invite, but I need to get to work. I already clocked in."

"Suit yourself. Always gotta be the do-gooder." Tom turned his back to Gary, signaling disdain.

As Gary continued toward his office, he heard snickers and a few loud guffaws echo from the group of men. He prayed silently as he walked, "Lord, give me strength to do what will honor you and help others."

Christy fell in step beside him as he finished the prayer. "Do you want to grab a cup of coffee with me?"

"Thanks, but I drank some at home."

They arrived at the desk, but Christy hesitated while Gary settled in. "I've been meaning to ask if you want to have lunch sometime?"

Gary's fingers froze on the keyboard where he'd entered his password. His thoughts jumped into hyperdrive. "Stay calm. It's an innocent request. Lunch won't hurt anyone; it's harmless. But be honest, you do think she's cute. Besides, what would Denise think? How would you feel if your wife had lunch with a guy she thought was cute? And remember Joseph. Look at the trouble Potiphar's wife caused him."

"I appreciate the offer, Christy, but my wife and I have an agreement. Thanks for asking, though."

Christy's face turned red, and she flounced away.

Gary pulled up the report he needed to finish and wiped unhealthy guilt from his mind. Though he didn't want to embarrass her, Christy's heart wasn't the one he vowed to protect. Denise held that honor.

Forty minutes later, Gary e-mailed the finished report to Mark, the CFO of First Capital Mortgage. Two days early. He helped one of the guys finish up a big project, then started the research for a presentation Mark wanted him to work on next. Engrossed, Gary worked five minutes into his break. The vibration of his iPhone alerted him Denise was calling.

Gary pulled the phone from his pocket. "Hi, honey, what's up?"

"I got a hold of the plumber, and he can be at the house tomorrow. Can you take off?"

"I don't think it will be a problem. I'll talk to Mark and make sure. I've got a presentation to prepare, but I can work on it from the house. I'll call you at lunch and let you know."

"How much do you think it will cost?"

"Probably not more than a couple of hundred, but don't worry, we can always pull from our emergency fund if necessary."

"Good. Don't forget, Emma's got practice until five, so I'll be home shortly after. I'd appreciate it if you could start supper. There's a casserole and the makings of a salad in the fridge."

"No worries. I'll see you at home. Love you."

"Me too. Bye." The line went dead.

Gary stretched his legs, stepped out to breathe some fresh air, then went back and jumped into the research again. He hardly noticed when Mark walked up to his desk.

"Can I see you in my office?"

Adrenaline coursed through Gary's veins. "Sure. Do I need to bring anything?"

"No. I'll meet you there in five."

Mark walked away and dread caused Gary's racing heart to skip a couple of beats. He rattled off a mental list of projects to himself and found everything either finished or well on its way. He double-checked the planner on his phone to make sure he didn't miss anything, but again, all seemed in order. But Gary knew deep cuts were in the making. Their business suffered from the financial barrage of a nation in distress.

Like a man walking death row, Gary made his way to Mark's office. Outside the door, he tapped.

"Come in," Mark said in his matter-of-fact manner.

Gary entered and sucked air when he saw Connie, the human resource manager, sitting next to an empty chair. Without uttering a sound, he walked into the room, noting a lack of oxygen around him. Connie nodded toward him in silence while he held the armrests and eased into the seat.

"Gary, we have to make cuts. There's no way around it. Positions must be eliminated."

Gary squirmed, and the chair squeaked beneath him. "I understand."

"I'm not sure you do. I asked Connie to bring your personnel file." Mark patted a manila folder lying on his desk. "Your record is spotless. From my own observation, you keep your head down and do whatever I ask. I can count on you to get any job done well and on time. You take initiative, but don't step beyond your authority level. Most notably, I don't see evidence of money or time wasted, especially with office gossip. Even your travel expenses come in thirty percent lower than others. This company could use more employees like you."

Instant heat caused Gary's face to flush. "Thank you, sir."

Mark continued, "In the last three years, we've only had two complaints about you."

"You did? What for?" The words slipped from Gary's mouth of their own accord.

"Nothing to worry about. Trivial and unfounded claims. It turns out both were driven by the same individual. He was misguided enough to think the way to get ahead was by making you look bad. It backfired. He's no longer with us.

"For a time, the accusations made me question you, but your actions proved you're a man I can count on."

Gary's thoughts flew to the man Mark referred to. He was a game-player. As a result, Mark rode Gary hard for several months, but when Gary thought he'd reached breaking point, it stopped. The other man ended up losing his job. Suddenly, Gary realized Mark was talking again.

". . . sorry about that. But it taught me a lesson. There's something different about you, and we'd like to tap into that potential. We can't know what the future holds, but if someone of your caliber would teach your secrets to our other employees, we might flip this downturn up. You've proven yourself trustworthy. We need help. And I think you're the right man for the job. What do you say?"

Gary wrestled with how to answer. He wasn't sure of the question. He decided on straightforward. "Pardon me, but I don't understand what you're asking."

Mark chuckled and leaned forward, his fingers interlocked over Gary's employment file. "That's one of the things I like, you're not afraid to clarify. I'm offering you a promotion of sorts. I can't give you a raise at this time, but where others are let go, you still have your job. I'd like you to work with human resources to retrain those we keep and start new hires off on the right track. Are you interested?"

Gary's shoulders softened and he expelled air he didn't realize he'd held. "Yes, sir, I am interested. You can count on me."

"Great. Connie, can you get things rolling?"

"Yes, sir."

Mark stood, signaling dismissal of the meeting. He extended his hand across the desk. "I expect good things. Don't let me down. And one of these days, I'd like to find out what makes you different."

Gary kept his eyes on Mark's while he lowered his head slightly, pursed his lips, and shrugged his shoulders. "I try to be a Joseph. I ask God to bless our company through the work of my hands."

"Hmm, interesting. Maybe we can schedule lunch and you can tell me more."

Gary pumped his boss's hand. "It would be my pleasure. Thank you for the opportunity," he said, then walked out behind Connie.

Gary couldn't wait to tell his wife. He missed Connie's small talk as he followed her to her office, distracted in a silent prayer of thanks.

Today's job market is tough. With heroic effort, employees who choose God's way refuse to justify inappropriate behavior. Heroes don't offer excuses, and they're not blinded by entitlement. Heroes remember they were hired to earn a paycheck, not simply collect one. Heroes don't waste their employer's money; instead, with integrity, they work the same whether someone can see them or not.

As you read on, I urge you to conduct your own fact-finding missions. At the end of each chapter, you will answer three investigative questions designed to help you decide whether you are taking every precaution to protect your job, your family, your employer, and our economy. Can the Joseph Factor improve your life?

Follow your dreams and leave justification behind. Answer the investigative questions and dare to be different. Become irreplaceable. Become a leader. But remember, great men and women first learn to follow in humility.

———————— Investigative Questions ————————

1. Do you labor for profit or does mere talk lead you to poverty? (Prov. 14:23).

2. Do you work as working for the Lord, not for men, since you know that you will receive an inheritance from the Lord as a reward? (Col. 3:23–24).

3. Is your behavior excellent among your co-workers so that because of your good deeds, as they observe them, you glorify God? (1 Pet. 2:12).

Chapter 2

The Ruth Return

A great leader must first
follow a great distance.

The world says, "Work smarter, not harder. Listen to your truth. The Inner You knows more than anyone else what's good for you. Look out for number one. Be a leader, not a follower."

But what happens if no one is willing to follow? Don't we bump heads and chests, losing time to ongoing conflicts over who's right and who's wrong? Can't we lose valuable information when we disregard the wisdom of people who walked ahead of us?

The types of messages listed above shift thought patterns so employees believe they know more than their peers. When we think more highly of ourselves and assume we know more than our predecessors, we become permanently disgruntled. Never satisfied or content, we run ahead of our leaders. Our jobs are in jeopardy. An uncoachable employee doesn't benefit the team.

In today's society, impatience drives many of us to miss an important element of growth. So often, a new hire wants a position at the top to springboard ahead of the pack. Followers are seen as weak.

Whether you sweep floors or are an executive in a Fortune 100 environment, there are life lessons you can learn from your job.

Whether you stay with the company and make it a long-term career, or it's a summer job to earn money for your first car, this position has purpose. A great leader first must follow a great distance.

Jack Nichols said, "Every person I work with knows something better than me. My job is to listen long enough to find it and use it." Many of today's new hires think they know more than every person they work with. They believe other people should listen to them. But following the right example can glean great results.

Too many new hires think practical help is beneath them. They believe that to ask questions, take notes, make samples to follow, or use other simple tools makes them look bad on the job. In my experience, someone humble enough to admit a need for help is more valuable than someone who does the job poorly because of foolish pride. We have two ears and one mouth for a reason—so we can listen twice as much as we speak.

A humble willingness to learn is not a sign of weakness. It's far worse to walk through life labeled with a bad attitude, arrogance, and other negative traits. We are defeated before we start and fail to recognize it. No amount of masking hides the truth of an unteachable spirit.

Ashley's ambition shows how a desire to overcome adversity, filtered through impatience, can result in negative consequences. Her tale teaches us the value of a willing heart.

Diploma gripped in hand, Ashley's smile shone through eyes colored with teal-green contacts. She shook the dean's hand and then swept a honey-toned bang off her right eye. Determination had propelled her to the top of her class, and she strode, chin up, toward the exit. The scent of triumph seemed to emanate from the vases of blue and gold carnations scattered across the stage. At the final step, she lifted the paper above her head in a victorious salute.

After the speeches were finished, graduation caps sailed through the air. Mindy, Ashley's best friend, turned and hugged her tight.

"Time to celebrate. Let's go party." Snippets of Mindy's dark hair got in Ashley's eye.

Ashley pulled away from the embrace and said, "I promised Mom I'd eat dinner with her first. I'll meet you at the party later. But I can't stay long. My interview's in the morning, and I don't want to blow it. This is my shot."

Anxiety clouded Ashley's thoughts. She'd fought hard to make something of herself, and success was within reach.

"Relax. A little less work and a lot more play wouldn't hurt you. We're twenty-two, not forty-two." Mindy grinned. "We've got the rest of our lives to tackle the world."

"I know what I want and waiting isn't an option."

"Whatever. I still think you should learn to relax." Mindy grabbed another quick hug and then turned without waiting for a response. She offered a wave with the back of her hand and disappeared into the crowd.

Ashley stood alone. Her best friend didn't know that telling Ashley to relax was like telling her not to breathe. She went to dinner with her mom but never did make it to the party.

The next morning, there was no ringing alarm or sun-drenched rays; only dark silence greeted Ashley when she awoke. Her adrenaline pumped hard as she flung blankets back. She made her bed and headed to the tiny bathroom in her apartment to pop in colored contact lenses. After a quick shower, she smoothed her blonde hair into a serious-looking bun on the back of her head. Carefully applied taupe eye shadow accented her teal eyes.

She walked to the closet and scanned the rows of hangers positioned in precise order, according to color and clothing type. Ashley's fingers rested on a chocolate skirt and jacket; she knew the polished fabric would accent her body in a professional style. A sage green blouse and chocolate-colored pumps finished the tailored effect.

Ashley glanced at her watch and groaned. More than three hours before her appointment. The Carter Grand was a five-minute walk from her apartment, a strategic move when she first set her sights on the hotel chain. Months of walking past its luxurious entry, spying the sparkle of marbled floors, made her ache for that kind of life.

With a sigh, she grabbed the portfolio on her nightstand and went to the kitchen. She flipped the light on and plucked a container of yogurt and a bottle of water from the refrigerator. Ashley sat down and ate at her breakfast nook while looking over Carter International Inc.'s history and stats for the umpteenth time.

Ashley read from chocolate and sage stationery. Having done her homework, she knew that everything with Carter's name displayed its trademark color scheme. Her well-chosen outfit mirrored their brand image. The upscale hotel and resort chain was known for high-end amenities and high-class clientele. Successful people stayed at Carter. Successful people worked there.

Opportunities for travel, glamor, and adventure fit Ashley's ambitions well. She chose her education based on the Carter model. Years of planning and preparation suited her for a career in the industry, and she knew she was perfect for the current opening as the Carter Grand hospitality manager.

Ashley squirmed and looked at her watch again. Subtle strands of sunrise filtered through her kitchen curtain. Within hours, she hoped to shine as well.

Finally, it was time. A few steps before the entrance to the Carter Grand, Ashley shifted the folder in her hand, stopped, and breathed deeply. Simmering restaurant bacon, mingled with car exhaust and fresh cut grass, gave her an instantaneous ache on each side of her temples. She tugged at the edges of her jacket, straightened her spine, and allowed the doorman to usher her inside. Ashley knew exactly where she was going.

The mahogany concierge desk was staffed by a dark-haired woman of slight build. Her translucent complexion made her black eyes appear bold. With a voice as rich as her flawless face, she asked, "May I help you?"

Ashley cleared her throat. "I'm here to see Mr. Rushing. I have a nine o'clock appointment."

"Certainly." The aristocratic woman breezed her left hand toward a discreet waiting area. "If you'd like to have a seat, I'll let him know you've arrived."

Ashley sat, cautious to cross her legs in a demure fashion, tucked slightly beneath her plush chair. Every move rehearsed—every motion intended. She opened the portfolio and scanned its contents again.

Her appointment time came and went. Twenty minutes past the scheduled interview, Ashley tapped her fingers in irritation. *How rude. I certainly wouldn't conduct business in such an unprofessional manner.*

Fifteen minutes later, she approached the concierge. "I'm sorry to bother you, but could you check with Mr. Rushing? My appointment was thirty-five minutes ago."

The woman, unruffled by Ashley's frustration, nodded her head and calmly pushed a button. "Could you tell Mr. Rushing his nine o'clock is still waiting?" She listened, and smiled into the telephone receiver. "I will. Thank you." She hung up and looked at Ashley with warmth in her onyx eyes. "Mr. Rushing's administrator asked me to convey his apologies. He hopes to be with you shortly and wants to thank you for your patience."

Dismissed, Ashley flounced back to her seat, forgetting to move as rehearsed. For the next thirty minutes, she glared and squirmed, furious at the insult of waiting so long.

Finally, a semibald man wearing an expensive suit approached. He stood mere inches taller than Ashley and looked nothing like she envisioned. He extended a manicured hand. "Ms. Beck, I'm Sam Rushing. Sorry to keep you waiting."

Ashley rose to meet him, accepting the handshake. "I'm happy to meet you." Anxiety replaced her annoyance.

"Let's go to my office and we'll get started." He turned and she followed him into a gleaming elevator.

When they stepped off, Ashley swallowed hard. Thick, soft carpet cushioned her feet. The understated scent of cinnamon drifted throughout the room. A stunning woman seated at an immaculate desk worked on a computer. Five-foot granite urns, filled with fresh roses and lilies, stood as bright centurions, guarding massive, polished doors.

Mr. Rushing turned to his administrative assistant. "Barb, can you hold my calls for the next hour?" Then he turned one of the knobs and invited Ashley to enter. The smells, sounds, and sights of success were everywhere. Sam Rushing walked across the expansive office and sat behind a sprawling piece of dust-free furniture. He motioned for Ashley to take one of the leather chairs across from him. "Now, Ms. Beck . . ."

"Please, call me Ashley."

"Okay. Tell me, why do you want a career with us?"

Ashley clutched her portfolio, and ran down the list of memorized qualities she'd found on the Carter website. She didn't breathe until she recited the last item.

Mr. Rushing leaned forward and smiled. "Well, you're definitely familiar with what we want, but my question is, 'What do you want? Why do you want to work for us?'"

Ashley felt her face flush. "I majored in hotel management and wrote my thesis on Carter International. I've studied what makes a great leader, and I've got ideas to help your team grow."

The executive chuckled. "So you want to be a great leader? But do you understand what the job demands? Are you willing to do whatever it takes to learn?"

"Absolutely. I know I'll be an asset."

"Then I have a position to offer you. It's how I got my start."

Ashley glanced at the wall to her right, full of framed certificates, and photos of Sam Rushing with celebs. She held her breath. The promise of her dream was about to become reality.

"If you're interested, I'll send you to human resources and we'll start the paperwork today. You can begin training tomorrow. Report to the kitchen in the morning at 8 A.M. sharp, and Phil, our head chef will teach you the ropes."

Ashley's face turned cold as the blood drained. Her heart thundered in her chest. "Sir, I don't understand. The kitchen?"

Mr. Rushing leaned back in his chair and rocked slightly. "Is there a problem?"

"No, sir, but I think you misunderstood. I'm interviewing for the hospitality manager's position."

"Actually, I understand what you need. But I'm not sure you do. Your education is a good thing, but there's nothing like on-the-job training. There's no better way to develop leadership skills than to follow great leaders. Phil is one of our best. Learn from him and you won't go wrong."

"But he works in the kitchen." Ashley heard the whine in her own voice and shuddered.

"Yes, he does, and so will you if you want a career with Carter International. I'm offering you the chance to start on the ground floor. You won't begin as a manager; you aren't ready yet, but you can work your way through the ranks one department at a time. You cannot lead in an area you haven't traveled. Are you willing to follow? The choice is yours."

With tears pooling in her eyes, Ashley stood. "Thank you, but working in a kitchen won't make use of my education or my talents. I have a lot more to offer. I appreciate your time."

Mr. Rushing walked around his desk and escorted Ashley back to the brass doors. He stopped and faced her. "If you change your mind, give me a call. I wish you the best." Then he turned the knob, took her back down the elevators, and left her in the lobby where their doomed meeting began.

In that moment, Ashley felt like years of her life were wasted, preparing for something that just slipped through her clenched fists. She stepped past the doorman and wandered home in a blur of bitterness. The blast of city sounds surrounded her, but Ashley didn't notice. She was lost in self-absorbed thought. It would take years of grinding away and getting chiseled down before she saw Mr. Rushing's offer as a gift.

———

Many people get close but never seem to close the deal on a job they really want. Often, they shake their heads in wonder, trying to figure out what happened. They don't realize the subtle influence of the world's success plan undermines their dreams.

Some are hired but are the first to go when necessary layoffs begin. A pattern of behaviors they can't see in themselves snatches away their job security. They pretend to listen, but they really believe they can outsmart others. When asked to demonstrate instructions they've been given, too often they are stumped, and, instead of looking smart, they end up looking foolish.

God's way protects us from ourselves. He teaches us that we are irreplaceable when we follow the right example. Regardless of our ambitions, in order to achieve them, we must learn to follow godly examples a great distance. We are the difference the world needs when obedience guides our steps.

My own career path started, and continues, in great humility. I have no college degree. But by God's grace, I've been given the gift of prosperity in every position I've held. From my first job as an unpaid babysitter, I moved on to a housekeeper and became a fast-food waitress. I graduated to department store clerk, worked in a convenience store, was a factory worker and banker, and made my way as a sales rep. I started a successful bookkeeping business until I came to manage one of the country's largest river resorts. Today, I'm privileged to teach others how to work efficiently and with integrity. Jesus is the secret to my success.

I didn't necessarily enjoy every job I had. But I reminded myself that I was paid the same, no matter what they asked me to do. Had I turned up my nose at any one task, I would have missed opportunities to gather valuable tools that equip me for success today. If I failed to follow, I could not lead.

I'm amazed when I hear a statement such as, "You won't catch me working fast food. Those jobs are for losers." To believe a particular position is beneath you means to risk missing growth opportunities. Too many people turn down the chance to accumulate tools that would help them later in their career. Some spend their entire lives never getting ahead, because they aren't willing to walk humbly behind another.

Ruth from the Old Testament is a prime example of someone who didn't get ahead of herself or others. She followed someone older and more experienced into a land of unknowns. She listened and applied the godly wisdom her mentor offered. She possessed qualities that destined her for success. Her choices changed history. As a result of her humility, Ruth became irreplaceable.

Let's trace the facts that set her apart.

- Despite facing an unknown future, Ruth agreed to follow Naomi, an older woman with more experience, and Naomi's God. She committed herself to service, no matter what. She followed with complete determination (Ruth 1:14–18).
- Ruth offered to invest her labor for the benefit of both women. Her motives were pure, and she worked steadily, only taking a short rest (Ruth 2:2–7).
- When Boaz offered provision and protection, Ruth accepted with humility and followed his instructions (Ruth 2:8–14).
- Ruth worked until evening and then refined her labor. She shared the results with her mentor and held nothing back (Ruth 2:17–21).
- Ruth did everything as she was told (Ruth 3:5–6).

Because she did exactly as instructed, because she was willing to follow, Ruth ended up in a place of honor. Her legacy as King David's great-grandmother also meant her bloodline passed through to include the King of kings, Jesus Christ. Can you imagine if one strand of DNA were altered in the genetic code? The world as we know it would be totally different if Ruth hadn't humbled herself and worked hard. She was irreplaceable.

But can we apply Ruth's example to Ashley's situation? Is there any reason to think following a similar pattern would benefit a young woman with ambitions as old as time? Let's take another look at Ashley's life and see whether the principles from Ruth would make a difference in her modern-day story.

———

Ashley clutched her diploma as Mindy draped her in a huge hug. The pomp and circumstance behind them, the two friends made plans to meet up at the postgraduation party with their classmates. Ashley squeezed her friend tight before linking arms with her mother and heading to an early dinner.

Once seated at the restaurant, they placed their orders and settled in to celebrate.

Her mom reached across the table and clasped Ashley's hand. "I'm proud of you. It hasn't been easy since we lost Dad, but your hard work paid off."

At the mention of her father, Ashley's throat constricted. Her words squeaked with emotion. "You set a good example."

"I couldn't have made it without you. But now it's time for you to strike out on your own. Promise you'll stay true to your roots, and remember the things I taught you."

Ashley sighed, "You make it sound like we won't see each other again. I graduated college; I'm not moving across the country."

"Who knows what will happen after your interview. They might want to send you out of the country. This is your dream job. You can't pass up an opportunity."

"I don't want to leave you. Remember? Where you go I will go, where you stay I will stay."

Ashley's mom squeezed her fingers. "Your loyalty amazes me. But even Ruth left Naomi to follow the harvesters and glean in the fields. Go ahead. Work hard and follow your dreams. You have my blessing."

The next morning, Ashley woke before sunrise. After dinner with her mom, she'd met Mindy and their classmates at the party but still made it to bed by ten. In the predawn stillness, adrenaline pumped Ashley's heart into rapid beats. She used the energy to ask God to guide her through the promise of an important day. She made her bed, careful to smooth each tiny wrinkle.

After a warm shower, Ashley arranged her honey-colored hair into a polished bun at the back of her head. She plucked every strand of blonde from her brush, threw them in the trash can, and aligned the handle in a straight line on the pristine vanity. Brown eyes twinkled below taupe-accented lids. Now for the finishing touches.

After donning a silk blouse, tailored suit, and pumps matched to the Carter International color brand, Ashley went to the kitchen. She had plenty of time to prepare.

Sunrays, diffused through pale curtains, highlighted shades of chocolate-brown and sage on the portfolio sitting to her left. But over yogurt and water, Ashley settled in with her Bible. She opened to the book of Ruth and allowed herself to get lost in study and prayer for the next hour and a half.

Twenty minutes early, Ashley stood outside the large foyer of the Carter Grand. "This is it. Lord, you lead and I'll follow," she said out loud. With a straightened spine, Ashley stepped inside and strode across the gleaming marble floor to the concierge desk.

An elegant woman looked up and smiled. "May I help you?"

"I have a nine o'clock appointment with Mr. Rushing."

"Certainly." The woman spread her hand toward the waiting area tucked behind her. "Have a seat. I'll tell him you've arrived."

Ashley followed the direction of the woman's outstretched arm and sat down in a plush chair. While waiting, she opened the portfolio and scanned the pages again. Periodic glances at her watch confirmed the scheduled time came and went. Impatience tried to rear its head.

On the outside, Ashley forced herself to smile. Inside her mind, she reviewed Ruth's life from the earlier study. How did Ruth feel as she followed Naomi into a foreign land? When the dust choked her throat, as they walked thirty to sixty miles along rugged and steep terrain? Did she feel afraid and think about turning back? After the first of a seven-to-ten-days' journey on foot, did she want to run ahead of her mentor in frustration? Weakened by hunger, did she question Naomi's wisdom and wonder whether there wasn't a better way?

Ashley closed her eyes and imagined walking in Ruth's shoes, her mouth parched by a high desert sun in the afternoon. Acacia berries, plundered from wild trees, were the main nourishment for her starved body. The scent of eucalyptus and cedar was thick in the dry air she swatted to escape biting insects. At night, she and her mother-in-law camped in caves or huddled together behind shrub trees to hide from predators and keep each other warm. Lying awake in the dark, wide-eyed and anxious, she wondered about the unknown ahead. As the days passed and fatigue settled deeper in her bones, Ruth clung to her vows. One obedient step at a time, she would not forsake her promise to follow Naomi, no matter what.

If Ruth could endure, then so could Ashley. She opened her eyes and met those of a medium-sized man with a balding head, cocked in a curious stare directed her way. His expensive suit spoke of importance.

"Ms. Beck, I presume?"

Ashley knew by the fiery feeling on her neck that splotches of crimson stained her cheeks. "Please call me Ashley."

"All right then. Nice to meet you." He offered a manicured hand. "I'm Sam Rushing. Sorry I've kept you waiting so long."

She accepted his handshake. "It's no problem."

"Shall we get started?" The older man turned and walked toward the elevator.

Ashley boarded with him, and the purr of the motor whooshed them to a posh, private suite. "Oh," slipped from her mouth as deep piled carpet surrounded her feet. The scent of fresh roses and lilies mingled pleasantly with a touch of cinnamon. Every fixture and piece of furniture sparkled.

"Ashley, this is Barb," Mr. Rushing said, introducing Ashley to his administrative assistant.

"Nice to meet you."

The executive stopped at his office door. "Hold my calls for the next hour please," he said, then turned the knob and ushered Ashley inside.

The interior of his office reflected the impressive ambience found throughout the entire Carter Grand building. Mr. Rushing pointed to a leather chair across from his desk. "Please have a seat."

The leather whispered as she sat, legs tucked beneath her.

Sam Rushing went straight to the subject. "Why do you want a career with Carter International?"

Ashley clutched the portfolio and thought of the information listed on the company website. Ruth also touched her thoughts. "I majored in hotel management and wrote my thesis on your organization, but my real motivation is to learn from great leaders. I lost my dad six years ago. It taught me the value of leaving a legacy, so I want my life to make a difference. Your company has a reputation for service leadership."

Sam Rushing leaned closer. "Sounds like you've thought this through. Tell me, what makes a great leader?"

"A great follower." Ashley relaxed under the warm encouragement in Rushing's voice. His gentle questions drew her into sharing her current hopes and future dreams. When she finished, he leaned back and rocked for a few moments. Ashley didn't flinch while she waited for him to say something. Finally, he spoke.

"If there's one thing I appreciate, it's healthy ambition mixed with a humble heart. So, you want to learn from great leaders?"

"Yes, sir."

"I have a perfect position for you. It's how I got my start."

Ashley stopped breathing.

"If you're interested, I'll send you to human resources today. You can begin training tomorrow morning at 8 A.M. sharp. Report to Phil, our head chef, in the kitchen."

Ashley scrambled to remember whether she'd clarified her desire for the hospitality manager's job. She gulped, "Sir, did you realize I'm interviewing for the management position?"

"There's no mistake. I understood, but I believe in on-the-job-training. You said it yourself, there's no better way to develop leadership skills than to follow great leaders. You can't take someone where you haven't been. You can't teach what you don't experience. I started my career in the kitchen and worked every area from laundry to front desk."

"So is this a management-trainee position?"

"You could say that. Unofficially. Officially, you will be hired as kitchen staff. We'll see how things progress from there. Do you want the job?"

Ashley looked down and squirmed against the soft leather. Silence lay heavy for several moments. The young woman squared her shoulders and looked up with a decisive glint. "I'll take it. I want to prove myself, and I'll work hard, no matter what position you place me in."

"That's the spirit." Mr. Rushing came around the desk and shook Ashley's hand with vigor. "I have a feeling you will fit in well around here. Now, let's get you to human resources."

After the new hire paperwork was complete, Ashley walked outside and stepped onto the city sidewalk. Horns blasted, car exhaust assaulted her, but she felt energized. On the walk home, she thought about perspective. She could choose to see this job as an insult or as a gift. She chose the latter.

For twelve years, Ashley Beck gave her best to every job she held at Carter International. One step at a time, she followed others and let her on-the-job education lift her to the top. Until one day she once again sat in Sam Rushing's former office.

Ashley's administrative assistant buzzed to say her nine o'clock had arrived. She stood and walked around the massive desk. The elevator took her downstairs to meet the potential employee. Ashley's heels clacked across the sparkling marble floor. Who knew, this could be the company's next great leader. Ashley smiled and extended her hand.

———

You cannot become irreplaceable until you follow the right example. A godly person who works with integrity whether seen or unseen looks different in the workplace—someone who puts one foot in front of the other until she finishes what she starts. Who enjoys the relief and celebration of a job well done. Someone energized to tackle the next project.

Can the Ruth Return teach you to follow God's way and work his success plan? I believe it can, but answer the investigative questions and try it for yourself.

Blaming others is another silent killer of career dreams. But a repentant heart can turn things around. Godly discipline turns lives of ash into crowns of beauty when we admit our faults, accept the consequences, and repay what we've taken.

─────── Investigative Questions ───────

1. Do you follow the example of those who follow Christ? (1 Cor. 11:1).

2. Do you remember as iron sharpens iron, so does one person sharpen another? (Prov. 27:17).

3. Do you think of yourself more highly than you ought to without thinking of yourself with sober judgment in accordance with the faith God has distributed to each of you? (Rom. 12:3).

Chapter  3

The David Discipline

Personal issues don't wait at the door,
they follow you inside.

In today's society, pretense drapes every aspect of work. We dare not tell anyone if we struggle. Cloaking our problems, we pretend to have it all together, especially on the job. And we delude ourselves into thinking this will make us irreplaceable.

If a supervisor smells weakness, you might be passed over for the next promotion. If depressive tendencies haunt you, you're labeled inferior. Unresolved grief is best kept to yourself. Anger is better hidden than expressed. And God forbid you are bold enough to mention feeling overstressed about a project or process. You might get a raised eyebrow, skeptical glance, or bad evaluation.

Even our world of communication offers a safe haven for those who wish to hide. We talk via text, Facebook, Tweet, and video conference. We feel safer expressing ourselves on YouTube than in person. Through these faceless interactions, we find new places to shelter our true selves and honest needs.

In the loneliness, our desire to numb dark emotions increases. And we look for escape in all the wrong places.

Masking on the job is a protective measure, but in reality it prevents us from dealing with our problems so we can be truly effective. In turn, it affects any potential rewards we may receive from our employers. When we smoosh emotions like guilt, anxiety, and fear into the tiny crevices of our minds and souls, they build. But like volcanic magma, you can only force so much energy into small spaces before it begins to ooze out.

The more adept we become at cramming inner struggles, the more lava-like those bits and pieces become. Problems pile on top of problems, until they melt into each other and we can hardly identify the original source of our pain. The more our hidden emotions accumulate, the greater the pressure, culminating in an explosive release.

A bulge in our behavior may predict a future blast of violent energy; family members often feel the heat of smaller outbursts before the rest of the world sees the full impact. Yet even we are surprised when the explosion bursts.

We expel noxious fumes on some unsuspecting soul at work. We take our unhealed issues out on an innocent person. The magma of everyday stresses spurts into lava, and when things finally die down, a hard crust forms over our hearts. This is how we survive.

In my research, I found one of the most comprehensive lists of common stressors from the Health and Safety Executive, a government website by the United Kingdom.[1] Many of the items listed are often overlooked triggers that can impact our productivity in negative ways. An argument with a child at home, car trouble, moving, caring for a sick or elderly parent, a dirty house, calls from a bill collector, forgetting to plan for dinner, or a traffic jam on the drive in. Whether big or small, outside influences can throw us into despair and affect our work. In worst-case situations, our personal problems offer us an excuse to mask or influence our emotions by looking for escapes. We think we've covered well, when in fact our pain-filled reactions point to inner problems. Few dare say a word to us about the sulphuric attitudes seeping from our core.

One man's inner fury shows us how piling pent-up emotions on top of each other can affect more than work performance. Blaine's unprocessed grief is not uncommon in today's work environments.

Blaine clocked in and beelined toward his desk in the Quality Control office, head down. The greasy odor of machine parts, mingled with steady thuds from moving equipment, was causing the blossom of an early morning headache. Blaine hoped it wouldn't bloom into a migraine.

He hadn't even turned on the computer when Mike, one of the line leaders, walked up with a piece of metal in hand. He laid it on the desk. "Can you take a look at this? I think our stamp is offset."

Blaine punched his computer's power button. "Are you kidding me? I haven't had my first cup of coffee yet. You know I can't think clearly until at least nine or ten. It's gonna have to wait."

"But we could stamp over two hundred bad parts in that amount of time."

Blaine rubbed circles on his temples. "The setting could be fine."

"Or, we could waste a lot of material and man hours putting out poor quality. You're supposed to be the guy in charge of making sure that doesn't happen."

"You make the call then."

"It isn't my job," Mike said.

Blaine stopped rubbing and grimaced. "Can you at least let me get my computer going, and one coffee down? Thirty minutes, all right?"

Mike picked up the part, and slung it next to his side in a discus motion on his way out. He mumbled at the door, "If our quality manager doesn't care about our products, why should anyone else?"

The door shook on its hinges when Mike slammed it shut. The rattle of glass caused the migraine to sprout petals that unfolded around Blaine's head. He cringed as the metal file drawer screeched open. Reaching deep, he picked up two prescription bottles, opened one, and shook out three 40 mg Relpax tablets. The bottle recommended no more than one tablet at a time, with a maximum of two in a twenty-four-hour period.

Blaine worked up a small amount of spittle and swallowed without liquid. Then he got up and started a pot of coffee, though caffeine was on his migraine restriction list. While it brewed, he put the Relpax down and picked up the other bottle lying next to it.

He didn't slow down to read the label telling him how much Vicodin he could take. It didn't matter anyway—he needed more than other people. Since his motorcycle accident two years before, he was on a daily diet of painkillers.

He shook two into his palm, thrust them in his mouth, and snapped his neck back, so the chalky ovals would slide down his throat. Then he sat to trace fresh circles on his temples until the coffee finished perking.

Blaine was pouring when the phone rang, causing him to jump and scald the outer part of his hand holding the mug. He focused on keeping his grip, but the moment he got the pot on the warmer, he switched hands so he could wave and blow on his fingers. The office telephone continued to jangle with the sound of an outside call.

Cursing, Blaine slumped into his chair, and picked it up on the fourth ring. He spat, "Dakota Quality, Blaine speaking."

"Are you okay?"

The sound of his mother's voice stole what little energy he'd held onto. "Did you need something, Mom?"

"I haven't heard from you in almost a month."

"I've been busy."

"Too busy for your mother?"

Blaine groaned into the mouthpiece. "Don't start. I've already had a bad morning."

"I'm sorry. Well listen, I don't want to keep you, but I need your help."

"Of course." He didn't mean to sound so cynical.

"It's your father."

"What's new? Aren't you tired of fighting yet? It's not like you divorced yesterday."

His mother whined, "Did you know he's taking that floozy on a cruise? He never took me on a cruise. He never took me anywhere. I need you to find out how much he's spending."

"Are you serious?"

"Why wouldn't I be? The garage door on our house isn't working, and I think he should fix it. After all, I wouldn't be alone in this maintenance nightmare if he hadn't had an affair. He should offer to pay for some of the repairs. Why shouldn't he help? He owes me."

"Dad hasn't lived in that house for almost twenty years. He has no interest in it anymore, financial or otherwise. Call someone to fix it, or if you hate it that much, then sell it. You can do whatever you want, but Dad doesn't have any part in it."

Sniffles vibrated through the phone line and into the veins already pulsing throughout Blaine's head.

His mother exhaled dramatically. "Fine. Take his side. Forget that he didn't pay all your child support. Disregard the fact that you couldn't afford college. I only wanted you to find out how much he's spending on that silly cruise. He's not just stealing money from me, it's your money too, and he's spending it on that woman."

"I don't want in the middle of this mess. Leave the past in the past."

His mother's sniffles turned into sobs. "You always say that."

"You might consider listening, then."

"You're ungrateful."

The line clicked loud and buzzed dead like the sound of a flat heart monitor. Sometimes, Blaine wished his heart would stop, so he wouldn't have to deal with his life.

A glance at the computer screen told him more than thirty minutes had passed. He cussed, picked up his mug, and swigged a couple of times before leaving to face Mike. Round two coming up.

He hoped the drugs would kick in on the way to the fight. He grabbed his safety goggles and earplugs, then headed out to the floor.

FIRST HIRED, LAST FIRED

Even through the plugs, the thump of machinery bounced along Blaine's cranial nerves. He tapped Mike on the shoulder, and tried to smile when the line leader turned around. Must not have pulled it off.

Mike offered only a snarled expression, no words. He picked up the part and practically slammed it in Blaine's hands.

Blaine turned the offensive piece over a few times, and spotted a blemish. He motioned for Mike to lean in and shouted, "I see what you're talking about. Let me take a couple of measurements in my office. I'll be back in a few minutes." He tried another smile, but once again, Mike ignored it.

Blaine managed to gulp down the rest of his coffee and start a new cup while he carefully measured. Sure enough, the figures verified Mike's theory. The part didn't pass inspection, and Mike wouldn't let him off easy.

He got up to deal with Mike again, and spotted the Vicodin bottle on top of his desk. "Man, I'm losing it. The boss would put my hide out to dry if he saw this." He opened the squeaky file drawer, and slid the tawny bottle back into the dark corner he'd pulled it from.

As expected, Mike made a stink out of the delay in identifying the quality defect. He even called the assistant plant manager in, forcing Blaine to scramble for excuses. He tried to hide his irritation, but the manager called him out for having a bad attitude.

Blaine was sick of everyone climbing on his back. He endured enough pain, and these jerks were making it worse.

The end of shift didn't come early enough. But finally, Blaine was able to shut everything down, put his desk in order, and head to the time clock. He punched out, and avoided eye contact with all his co-workers. His surly frame of mind put him out of the mood to deal with idiots.

At home, Blaine pulled his beat-up old Chevy under the sagging carport and pulled the keys out of the ignition. He entered the dilapidated trailer, tossed his keys on the cluttered table, and headed toward the fridge. With everything against him, he needed help to relax. Especially after a day like today, he was grateful for a cool drink.

Blaine nestled into the recliner with a family-sized bag of Cool Ranch Doritos, a tub of French Onion dip, and several cold beers close at hand. The flutes of *Survivor*'s theme wafted from the tube. The soothing combination of drink, junk food, and an altered reality soon lulled his anger and helped him move beyond the sting of the day's stressors.

When a new theme song started, Blaine muted the sound on the television and reached clumsily for his cell. He had to train his eyes on the contact list so they would focus, and then he dialed the right number.

His dad answered on the second ring. "Hello, son."

"Hey dad, how are ya? Hear you're going on a cruise."

His dad's throat cleared. "Who told you that? Wait. Let me guess. Your mother."

"Yeah, she called me at work today. She's kind of steamed about it."

"It's none of her business."

"That's what I told her, but you know Mom. She got herself riled because the garage door opener isn't working."

"Tell her to call a repairman."

"I did. So, a cruise? Where'd you get the money for something like that?"

His dad sputtered a few unintelligible words before starting fresh. "Tammy, uh, got a bonus. She, um, well, if it wasn't for her job, we wouldn't be able to."

"Yeah, I figured it was something like that."

"Are you doing okay?"

"Great—great. Well, I've got some stuff to take care of, so I'll talk to you later."

"Good to hear from you, son. Call me soon."

Blaine wanted to say, "The phone dials both ways," but instead clicked off and dropped the phone on the armrest.

His dad always lied to him about money. Nothing new. When he walked out, he took all his support with him. Financial, physical, and emotional. Blaine had known nothing else since he was fifteen years old.

Blaine watched smoke curl from the orange tip of his cigarette as he inhaled. Exhausted, he fell asleep in the recliner less than an hour later.

The sound of blue jays bickering caused Blaine to move his groggy body. It took a few minutes for his brain to filter past the sun's brightness and realize he wasn't stretched out in his bed. Then something registered.

The alarm. He didn't hear the alarm. He vaulted out of the chair, snatched his cell phone off the armrest, and yelled out loud, "Argggghhhh, not again."

He ran to his room and pushed through the empty hangers in the hollow closet. In panic, he stumbled to the nearest pile of dirty clothes and grabbed a pair of jeans. He snapped them hard three times, to make sure most of the wrinkles smoothed out. He had to force the zipper shut, under the growing paunch of his belly.

Blaine rushed toward his chest of drawers—at least he should have a clean T-shirt. In his rush, he stepped on a plate slathered with half-eaten food from two nights ago. He slipped on the slick surface and flew into the air, coming down on his backside. He stood up massaging the tender tissue; it would definitely bruise.

He didn't baby himself too long but tugged the shirt over his head while peeking through the neck hole for a decent pair of socks on the floor. He found a navy and a black, close enough. Shoes untied, he snagged the car keys and ran out the door. If he didn't hit too much traffic, he might still make it on time.

At four minutes 'til, Blaine punched the clock. His head felt swollen, and his sullen outlook filled him with dread as he headed toward his office. He hated the stress his job caused. If he didn't have to come into this rat hole, life would be near perfect.

Down the aisle, Blaine noted the three-inch space between his door and its frame. "Stupid janitor left my door open," he grumbled.

But after a few steps closer, movement caught his eye, and he slowed his approach to a more cautious pace. He peeked around the door jamb and sucked air. Craig, the assistant plant manager, hovered over his computer and, even worse, held the bottles of Relpax and Vicodin. Blaine couldn't see who Craig was talking to, but Mike's voice gave him away.

Blaine leaned back. Rolls of bitter bile crawled up his esophagus. He thought about hurrying away, but it was too late.

Craig called out, "Blaine, come on in."

He eased inside, barely moving the door on its hinges.

"Can you explain these?"

"Relpax treats my migraines."

"And the Vicodin?" Craig shook the tawny containers, and tablets clicked against plastic. "How long have you been out of rehab?"

"Three months, sir."

"We've done everything possible to support you, but you aren't willing to help yourself. I told you last time was your final chance. It's obvious your prescription drug habit is affecting your work performance in detrimental ways. Clear out your desk."

"You can't fire me," Blaine spoke without thought.

"Your bad attitude, insubordinate habits, and unreliable ways are well documented. I've personally spoken with you numerous times. I am letting you go. I'll wait while you get your things."

Blaine called Craig a few choice words and then turned to spew his venom on Mike.

Mike's red face belied his calm tone. "You did this to yourself. You're on a mission to destroy yourself. Maybe if you stopped blaming the world for your problems, you could see what's in front of your face."

Mike brushed against Blaine's shoulder on the way out.

Blaine slammed his personal effects into the brown cardboard box sitting conveniently on his desk.

As Blaine was escorted from the building, Craig offered a final condolence. "Sorry it didn't work out, Blaine. I wish you the best."

Blaine rewarded him with an obscene gesture and name. He drove home believing everyone was against him and they were all idiots. He'd spend the rest of his life trying to outsmart them all and living the life of a fool as a consequence. His destitute lifestyle never equaled his arrogant words.

We all mess up. No matter our motive, efforts, or position, eventually, we will stumble. Maybe drugs or drink aren't the vice—after all, there is a long list of things people are addicted to today. Often, we become so used to feeling bad, we deny their damaging side effects.

Caffeine, negative attention, smoking, gambling, television, complaining, spending money, gossip, video games, inflicting physical harm to our bodies, sugar, power, all things Internet, texting, or sex can morph into addiction. Even things that are good for us like budgeting, medicine, competition, exercise, work, sleep, beauty products, or family and friends can become addictive if we use them as a cover.

Anything that takes us out of reality, even for a few moments, can make us ineffective.

So how do you start over when it seems like life conspires against you? What if your mistakes are so big that it appears God himself won't forgive? Will you allow guilt and anger to consume all your good potential?

David was a man with such a choice to make. Like many employees today, David failed to perform at the standard placed before him. In his case, the boss he answered to was God.

Placed at the highest position in his nation, king of Israel, David allowed a series of choices to lead him down a destructive path.

According to 2 Samuel 11, David foolishly and arrogantly failed to meet his obligation to go to war at the appointed time. Instead, he sent one of his subordinates to do the job.

In a state of complacency, he committed a grievous sin against people and God with a beautiful woman named Bathsheba. Bored because he failed to fulfill his true purpose, David distracted himself by wasting his power on immediate pleasure. If he hadn't neglected his duty, he couldn't have acted on the opportunity of great temptation.

When his decision wrought obvious consequences, Bathsheba's pregnancy, he tried to hide it by heaping greater sins on top of the original. God didn't miss a single act in the deceptive scenes playing out before his eyes.

For a time, it appeared as if David was literally getting away with the murder of his mistress's husband. (If you want to study an example of a man of pure integrity, up to his final breath, read the account of Uriah, Bathsheba's husband, in 2 Sam. 11:6–17.)

But David got away with nothing, for God had seen it all.

And I believe more than slaying a giant, leading successful armies, or conquering great nations, this is where David set himself apart. The details reflected in his attitude, once he knew he'd been found out, show us who the man truly was. A man described in the Bible as being after God's own heart. So what behaviors prove the purity of his motives? Let's take a look and see.

- Even as he attempted to hide his own wrongdoing, David couldn't shake his deep convictions about right and wrong (2 Sam. 12:5).
- David provided a specific formula for repaying those we've stolen from: restitution in the amount of four times what we've taken (2 Sam. 12:6).
- When confronted with accusation and proof of the offense, David rightly states, "I have sinned against the Lord" (2 Sam. 12:12–13).
- David accepted the punishment for his crime and submitted authority to the Judge who meted the sentence (2 Sam. 12:19–23).
- David returned to work. He no longer neglected his duty but, instead, rose to meet the challenges set before him.

He fulfilled his responsibility to the people who counted
on him, the nation of Israel (2 Sam. 12:27–29).

Remorse is a funny thing. When we confess in genuine repentance,
mercy follows. But if we insist on denial, we often get what our cynical
assumptions whisper—people are against us. David's example provides a clear formula for a fresh start.

Let's imagine how Blaine's life might differ if he were to let his
guard down and practice David's disciplines.

—◇—

The honk of the alarm vibrated through Blaine's migraine-laden head.
"Why do I have to do this?" He slammed his palm on the off button
and added to the pain reverberating inside his skull.

Blaine stumbled to the medicine cabinet and sleepily opened the
bottle of Relpax. Three tumbled onto his palm, and his throat tightened in temptation. Saliva started at his cheeks and pooled on his
tongue.

He shoved two of the pills back inside the bottle and turned the
lid in harsh determination. He sipped a small amount of water, swallowed the single migraine pill, and walked over to the table by his bed.
Blaine grabbed his *Twelve Steps and Twelve Traditions* book and
headed to the couch.

He read aloud as his fingers followed the words of Step 8, "Made a
list of all persons we harmed and became willing to make amends to
them all." Blaine closed his eyes, lifted the book, and laid it flat against
his forehead. A barrage of faces shadowed across his mind while he
breathed deep of paper and ink.

He lowered the book and read the passage two more times out
loud, and then laid the book aside so he could pick up the black leather-bound. He flipped to the bookmark, and the pages crinkled as he
opened to 2 Samuel 12. He read silently through verse 6, but something stopped him.

He backed up and read again. Then again. And finally, his voice cracked as he shared the words with an empty room. "He must pay for that lamb four times over, because he did such a thing and had no pity."

Shaking his head at the coincidence, Blaine held his fingers at the Bible's seam, while his free hand fumbled back to Step 8. His neck popped back and forth while he volleyed between books. The similarity was uncanny, and the message unmistakable. He'd heard other people talk about this kind of stuff, but it was the first time he experienced it for himself.

Blaine was convinced. God had spoken. He thought about it all the way to work.

On the job, his body still reacted physically to the sounds of crushing metal and the odor of petroleum-based machine products. Like a flipped switch, the sights, sounds, and smells made him ache for the soothing sensation of Vicodin. His muscles knew the habit that started with his motorcycle accident. But through extensive therapy, he was learning to deal with the temptation. One of the toughest problems Blaine resolved to face was that of his parents.

After extensive therapy with his Christian counselor, he visited his dad and mom individually. Starting with his father.

Blaine's dad invited him to sit on the couch, catty-corner from the recliner. Blaine looked around at the warmly decorated living room. An old string of resentment curled around his mind. But then he remembered something his counselor had said.

"Your father is probably hiding deep pain. You have to look past what you see on the surface. Just because he doesn't express fear or hurt, doesn't mean he isn't feeling them. You may not know about childhood wounds or other life experiences that have affected his decision making as an adult. Start cautiously, and talk through one thing at a time."

Blaine shifted his body forward, leaning closer to the recliner. "Dad, I've stuffed some things down into my soul, and I need to get them out."

Blaine's father pulled his head back, as if he'd taken a light punch. "Don't bring up the past. It's better left buried."

Blaine inhaled slowly through his nose. "I'm not here to condemn you, or make you feel bad. I simply need to clean out my own gunky emotions. I want a relationship with you, an honest one. I love you, and I need this. So I can heal. Hopefully, so we both can heal."

Blaine saw his dad's shoulders stiffen, but he didn't say no. Speaking slowly, Blaine determined to focus on one single point. He looked his dad in the eyes when he spoke. "Do you remember when I was four or five, and my pet rabbit died?"

His father nodded. "Her name was Queenie. Broke my heart to see you like that."

Knowing his dad connected to the memory made hope well up in Blaine. "When you moved out, it felt like Queenie died ten thousand times over."

The yellowy whites of his dad's eyes watered.

"I missed you so much. At fifteen, I didn't understand, so I tried to ignore the pain, and grabbed at anything to try and make myself feel better. I made some really dumb choices."

His father's neck shaded red. "I knew you'd get around to blaming me."

"That's not what I'm saying. I take responsibility for my own actions, and yet I also need to talk about what led up to those choices. I'd like to know how you felt when you left. I'm ready to listen—really listen. No bashing, finger pointing, or accusing anyone else. Just how you felt about the decisions you made. Did you regret any of it?"

A look of shock spread across his dad's face. "Of course I felt sorry that I hurt you and your mother. But I'm honestly not sorry I made the decision to leave."

Blaine gulped, wishing his dad had said he missed him, too, and feeling the sting of his father's truth. But Blaine resolved to listen fully—with head and heart—to his dad's response, knowing there was

probably much more beneath the words spoken. "I'd like to understand more about why you felt that way."

Blaine's dad shook his head back and forth, tiny tears now slipped
below his temples. "I can't deal with this right now. Can't we enjoy
being together again? Do we have to dredge up the past?"

Blaine stood up, walked to the recliner, leaned down, and gave
his dad a hug. "Let's take a break." He gently pulled away from their
embrace, stood, and let compassion lace his voice as he looked at his
dad's quavering body. "We don't have to do this all in one day. But
can we promise to deal with some of our buried pain, so it doesn't
continue keeping us apart?"

"Would you like to stay for supper?"

Blaine smiled, "It's a good place to start."

His dad stood, and clasped his hand on Blaine's shoulder. "I'm
glad you came, son."

Blaine's throat tightened. Father and son walked shoulder to shoulder toward the patio. Now if things would go this well with his mom.

When Blaine met with his mother, her initial resistance didn't
come as a surprise. But with persistent patience on his part, he finally
encouraged her to sit still and listen.

"You know how you tell me it hurts when people blow you off, or
act like you're being overly dramatic?"

"Yeah, but . . ."

Blaine bounced his pointing finger off his lips, making a gesture
that read, "Don't speak yet."

Her eyes widened.

"When you insist on bringing up your opinions about dad, it hurts
me. He's my father, and I don't think I'm the appropriate person for
you to vent with."

"But I don't have anyone else to talk to."

"That's why I'm seeing a counselor."

She huffed, "I don't need a shrink."

"Mom," Blaine gently chided. "My therapist doesn't shrink anything. He doesn't belittle me. He isn't trying to force his point. He simply lets me talk without interrupting, and asks me questions to help me arrive at my own answers. He cares without condescending."

"So you're saying I do that?"

"Don't put words in my mouth, and don't project your perceptions onto my experience."

"Sounds like shrink talk to me."

Blaine reached out and caressed his mother's arm. "If this is going to work, and I want our relationship to get better, not worse, we both need to listen fully. Deal?"

She melted under his loving touch. "All I've ever wanted is to be close. For you to know how much I love you."

"And I want the same. So let's start over."

It took months for Blaine and each of his parents to learn new ways of coping with past hurts. But over time, with careful steps, things improved dramatically. And Blaine knew it was time to apply those same lessons to his relationships at work.

On the way to Craig's office, nervous energy caused him to fidget. He tapped softly on the door when he arrived.

"Come in," the assistant plant manager bellowed.

Blaine crept through the door after turning the knob and lowered his head in a show of humility. "Sorry to bother you, but could I talk to you for a few minutes?"

"What's on your mind?" Craig scooted the stack of documents to his left and folded his arms on top of the desk. "Have a seat."

Blaine accepted the invitation to sit. "I owe you an apology, sir."

"Oh?" Craig's eyebrows elevatored up.

"I've stolen from you and this company."

Craig's face shaded to a ruby-like color. He leaned forward until his chest lay flush above his folded arms. Now only one eyebrow cocked. "What exactly did you take from me?"

"From the company, I've wasted a lot of time when I should have been working. I've also stolen a few office supplies." Blaine shifted in the chair. "From you personally? Respect."

"How's that?" Craig's eyes narrowed.

Now Blaine turned red. He wrung his fingers and looked down. "I've bad-mouthed you behind your back to other employees. My bad attitude influenced others to justify their own poor behavior." Blaine looked up remorsefully. "I'm truly sorry, sir. I plan to pay back four times everything I've stolen. It will not happen again."

Craig rocked his leather office chair forward and back. He palmed his hands together and touched fingertips to his lips. He spoke into his hands. "Why would you tell me this?"

"When I was in rehab, they forced me to deal with my life. I was furious at first, but over time I realized how much my parents' divorce, and continued feuds, started me down the road to escape. Over time, I traded as much reality as possible for the illusion of momentary feel-goods."

Craig stopped rocking.

"It boiled over when I had the motorcycle accident a few years ago. I got hooked on painkillers, and everything spun out of control.

"In therapy they didn't let me get away with hiding. When I stopped fighting and got to know about God, things began to turn around. I'm working the Twelve Steps and reading the Bible. This morning, I realized I needed to make amends for my theft. That's why I'm here—to start the process."

"That's quite a story."

"It's the short version."

"I admire your honesty. Maybe you can tell me the long version over coffee sometime."

"I'd like that." Blaine stood. "Before I go, I want to give you something." He took a squared paper out of his pocket and held it across the desk.

Craig accepted with a look of curiosity.

"This is my covenant with you. From today on, I promise to work with diligence and dedication. I promise to repay monetarily four times for the material possessions I stole."

"You don't have to go that far."

"I've sinned against God, and I owe it to him. Please allow me to fulfill my vow."

Craig shrugged, "If you insist."

"I also promise to restore the damage I've done to your reputation. I will build you up behind your back. I will speak no lies. And I will not participate in trash talk or justification. You have my spoken and written word."

Craig unfolded the paper and scanned the contents. Then he held out his hand in an offer to shake. "Thank you. I can honestly say this is a new experience for me. I have a feeling you're going to make it."

Blaine left and walked the plant floor toward his co-workers. He had a lot of other pieces of paper to give out. He smiled at the thought.

—⁓—

Everyone makes mistakes, but not everyone deals with them. Pride is an ugly beast humans fight. And pride is often the culprit that keeps us from reaching our greatest potential, an act with the power to transform our lives from mediocrity at best, and utter failure at worst.

Failures are not those who fall, but those who refuse to get up, face their problems, and deal with the consequences. No matter how things look on the outside, the truth of your success depends on how well you fail.

Emotions build like magma in a volcanic chamber. At the slightest conflict, a tremor can begin in our minds until lava explodes with a magnitude and velocity that allows it to splatter on people miles away from the eruption site.

Venting steam frequently reduces volatility. But how do you dig up things you've repressed so you can cleanse yourself from past poisons lurking in your subconscious? Create a Mind Map or write your own Story Board to relieve old pressures, prevent explosions at the wrong moment, and keep you from escaping to inappropriate places. I offer step-by-step examples of both processes on my website, www.brooksanita.com.

It is possible to rewrite the end of your own story.

He who has nothing to hide hides nothing. Becoming irreplaceable means digging down to old wounds and giving them the oxygen they need to heal. Don't avoid your problems—face them head-on and prepare for blessings as a result.

Often, the root of our behavior is words. The power to sting and the power to heal start at the sentences we speak. We should pay attention to what we say, because words do matter. In the next chapter, we'll look at those with the ability to make us irreplaceable and those that can cost us everything.

—————— Investigative Question ——————

1. Does concealment keep you from prospering? Or do you confess and renounce wrongdoing so you receive mercy? (Prov. 28:13).

2. Does wine no longer make you sing? Has your beer become bitter? (Isa. 24:9).

3. Are you weary and heavy laden? Do you need somewhere to find rest? (Matt. 11:28).

Chapter 4

The Jacob Jury

Words harness the power to move us
from mediocrity to meaning.

As an employer, I'm an observer. Sometimes I have to ask my employees, "Do you ever listen to yourself?" More often, I need to heed my own words, tone, and pitch.

Most people pay little attention to the meaning of language that falls from their lips. Gossip, broken promises, chronic complaints, rash texts, obscenities, and emotion-fueled social media are filled with careless words. I still catch myself falling into the dangerous trap of venting without thinking.

Rash statements can cost us our jobs. Irreplaceable people are careful with what they say.

Do you realize that telling someone, "I'll call you back in five minutes," is a promise?

My early training for any new hire, no matter their age, requires that I talk about promises. In today's hyperpaced culture, we throw quick answers at people so we can move on to the next challenge, activity, or escape. But seldom do we realize how many unfulfilled promises we make.

However, the person on the receiving end keeps track. Has someone ever told you they'd call you back in five minutes, and, even if you went about your day, a niggling frustration haunted you because of unfinished business?

If you've been told by someone, "Don't worry, I'll take care of it," don't you want to know it will actually be taken care of? And yet, how often do things fall apart?

Many promise makers respond with a blasé, "Sorry, I forgot." They don't consider how much time is lost. The emotional upheaval it causes someone else. Or at work, how much money it costs to revisit things because someone didn't keep their word.

But let the same person be on the receiving end of disregard or the perceived disrespect of waiting on someone else. As a manager, I hear about it all the time.

Unreliable employees say, "I'll do it," without considering the expectation they created. Irreplaceable employees follow up on every detail of the promises they make. Whether they use the word *promise* or not.

In my role as a leader, I work hard to express the importance of follow-through. Sometimes I ask employees who assume responsibility for a project, "Do I need to check back with you?"

"No, I've got it." So often spoken, and yet wisdom says check anyway.

Sadly, in most instances, the promise isn't kept. The work is half finished or poorly done. I have to force the employee to clean up the mess he or she created. And then I'm the bad guy. This is not a fun position for a manager, and the situation doesn't bode well for the employee who initiated it.

Want to become irreplaceable? Finish what you start, follow every detail, prevent the preventable, and ensure a manager's check will find all is well. Be an employee who values the words you offer.

Another unfortunate pattern in today's workforce is the propensity for chronic complaining. And those prone to this behavior are often the first to talk about others. No one wants to be around a negative person, and most people, at least those who wish to become irreplaceable, will look for ways to avoid them.

For those who choose to flock around juicy gossip and finger-pointing, the results are dangerous. Over time, humans tend to mimic the behaviors of those they spend the most time around. Who you hang with will determine how you hang. This means the negative follower in turn leads others in negativity. A poor attitude sours productivity and jeopardizes workers who wish to keep their jobs.

Russ, an administrative assistant at Leeholt Media Group, learned how subliminal influence from others could take him to places he never dreamed he'd go. His words altered his own course, but he didn't realize it—until it was too late.

—⁓—

Russ inhaled deeply as he turned the car off. He looked at his watch and muttered, "I may as well go in." Then he shoved his car door open to walk past rows of polished marble pots filled with red geraniums and jumbo yellow marigolds. The fresh-cut grass smelled like ripe melon. Russ waved at one of the landscapers who carefully clipped the leafy green shrubs bordering the face of a gleaming ground-level window at the base of the high-rise.

Russ stepped toward the revolving door and hesitated while the electronic reader signaled his presence and swished open. He shuffled in the semicircle, and then joined the shoe-clacking swarm who crossed the sparkling floor headed toward the elevators.

When Russ stepped off on the twenty-third floor, he walked down the corridor toward his office. Julie chirped from her receptionist's desk, "Good morning, how are you?"

"Fine."

"You don't sound fine." Julie scowled and turned back to her computer screen.

"Not everyone has a perfect life."

Julie snapped her chair around and squinted her eyes. "My life's not perfect, but I don't make my problems everyone else's. You might take lessons."

Russ was startled by the plucky outburst. Julie struck him as an empty-minded Barbie whose constant smile rubbed him the wrong way. He chose not to respond and rubbed his jawline until he sat down at his own desk. Forty minutes early.

Russ started writing the letter his boss, the vice president of radio marketing, had dictated the day before. He stopped typing to fume.

Julie's a suck-up. That's why all the big shots like her. She can afford to be bubbly. The only thing she does all day is answer the phone. She's got it easy.

A tap on the door interrupted his mental ranting. Jerry stuck his head horizontally around the door facing. "Hard at it already?"

"Don't remind me."

Jerry snaked the rest of his body into the room, stood up, and shoved his hands in his pants pockets. "You all right?"

Russ worked while he talked. "Yeah, just tired. My neck and shoulders are killing me."

"That stinks."

"I'm used to it."

"Maybe you should see a doctor."

Russ stopped typing. "I just need a new job. I work my tail off, and no one appreciates it. No matter what I do, it's never good enough. If I don't smile and pretend everything's hunky dory, I'm treated like I have the plague. My boss promised me a raise last month, but I didn't get squat. Why bother?"

Jerry's mouth turned downward. "I hear you. Did you say something to him?"

"It won't do any good."

"How do you know if you don't try?"

"I just know."

"Then why don't you send your resume out? Look for another job?"

"I'm not sure I can make the same money somewhere else. But I've thought about it. I'm sick of being treated unfairly because I don't bow down and kiss people's feet. By the time I get home, I'm too tired to deal with anything else. I don't have the energy to update my resume. This place takes it out of me."

"I know what you mean . . ." Jerry stopped short of their typical commiserations. The look of panic on Russ's face and quick no shakes of his head said someone now stood behind him.

Russ's boss, Don, clapped Jerry on the shoulder, and leaned around him to smile into the room. "Hey champs, ready to conquer the day?" He made a show of raising a fist into the air.

Russ didn't mean to roll his eyes, but he could tell he was busted by the reaction from across the room.

"Is there a problem?" Don dropped his arm and tightened his lips.

Russ tried to recover. "Sorry, battling a neck ache today."

"Again?" sarcasm spliced the awkward atmosphere. "I'll expect that letter in my in-box before eight. And I need the sales stats for the northwest region by nine thirty. You think you can handle that?" Don tugged on his necktie.

Russ widened his eyes and pasted a smile on his face. "Sure, I'll get them done."

"I won't ask twice." His boss spun away from the office.

"I'm on it," Russ raised his voice toward the hallway, hoping Don could hear him as he walked away.

"Whoa, he was mad," Jerry said.

Russ lowered his voice. "He's always blubbering about something and blaming me for it."

"I'd better let you get to it."

"I'm not worried. I can usually talk my way out of it. He won't do anything as long as I turn something in before the end of the day."

"He sounded serious to me."

"I know how to handle him. He should focus on a few of the other deadweights around here. Julie's a good example. She's got it easier than anyone, and yet everybody fawns over her."

Jerry looked down and scuffed the toe of his shoe across the carpet. "I thought she did a pretty good job. Have you watched her try to keep up with the phones, the VPs, and people calling for appointments?"

"Anybody can do that."

"Maybe. But I'm not sure I could juggle and keep my cool like she does." Jerry scratched his head.

"She's not that impressive."

"Guess not." Jerry rocked on his heels and lowered his chin.

Russ leaned forward on his elbows and splayed his fingers, digit against digit. "What about the rest of us? Don't we work hard?"

Jerry nodded, "It's true, we all deserve better. But I'd better get to work. My boss isn't so easily swayed." He tapped the door frame. "I'll catch you later."

Russ took his time on the letter and totally disregarded the sales stats. Off and on throughout the morning, he texted a few of his other allies in the building and groused. Although he did complete a lot of work, Russ stubbornly chose the things he felt like doing. He felt a sense of power as he put the final touches on the radio slots he'd scheduled for their newest client.

Right before three, Russ's boss stopped by.

"Oh, hey."

Don closed the door and walked solemnly to sit across from Russ. "Nine thirty came and went several hours ago. Where are my stats from the northwest?"

"Sorry." Russ hurried and picked the schedule off his printer. He held it out. "I finished the radio schedule for our new client."

Don took the report, and with a slow, controlled tone said, "I didn't ask you for this schedule by nine thirty. I told you I wanted the stats."

"I know, I tried, but the data wasn't that easy to find. I kept hitting stumbling blocks. I thought our client's schedule was important, too."

"I'll decide what's important." Don crumpled the edge of the paper in his hand.

Russ felt heat release and pulse through his veins. Hot and cold seemed to mingle inside his body. Danger bells rang in his head. He tried another tack. "I had trouble concentrating this morning because I didn't feel good. But I'm better now. I'll have it for you shortly."

Don stood up and moved behind the chair he'd been sitting in. "Don't bother. Jones got the information I needed."

"I didn't mean to let you down. I'll make it up." Russ also stood up.

Don gripped the back of the chair. "Jones got the promotion."

Ice stopped Russ's heart for a moment. "I've been here longer than him. I deserved that promotion."

"I'm tired of your mood swings and empty promises. You tell me what you think I want to hear and disregard what you don't want to do."

"I can change."

"Too late. The decision's made."

Over the next thirty-six months, Russ interviewed for several jobs, many paying much less than the one at Leeholt Media.

Things fell apart every time the interviewer asked about his current employment. When asked what he liked about the job, he could come up with few positive things to say. But when questioned about his dissatisfaction, many examples came to Russ's mind. Sadly, he didn't hear his own negative perspective and didn't realize how it sounded coming out of his mouth. Russ thought he masked the depth of his true feelings.

Potential employers, however, heard the heart that told on him.

With nowhere to go, Russ stayed longer than he wanted, though he was passed over numerous times, and eventually received a major demotion. He quit in anger and ended up getting a job he felt was far beneath him. The people in the checkout line cared little about his degree or qualifications.

Throughout the years, I've seen many people self-destruct from care-less words, spoken without meaningful thought. Our true feelings tell on us, sometimes sooner, as in a job interview, or later, after we get comfortable at work.

There's power in profanity and power in purity. One tears down, and one builds up. One makes us a warm body filling up space; one makes us irreplaceable.

If we focus on the failings of others, we cannot see our own. But if we think on the true, right, noble, and pure in those we work with, it can reduce our insecurities. We're strengthened to speak words that matter. Words we intend to keep.

Jacob was a man who learned the value of keeping his word. He made the choice to keep his promise long before he received benefits from it. He set his sights on a desired outcome, a woman he loved, and made decisions to take him to that end. Jacob made every choice through the filter of a life with Rachel. If an option wouldn't lead to that natural conclusion, he made a different decision. His example shows us how our focus and our words can take us where we want to go.

- Jacob agreed to work seven years for Rachel's hand in marriage. He kept his word and worked the full term (Gen. 29:18).
- Even when Jacob's father-in-law deceived him, by slipping Rachel's sister, Leah, in her place, Jacob agreed to work another seven years in exchange for the woman he truly wanted (Gen. 29:27).
- One week after Leah's bridal celebration ended, without fulfilling his promise to work another seven years, Jacob was allowed to marry Rachel (Gen. 29:28).
- Though Jacob had already received the outcome he desired, Jacob kept his word and worked another seven years (Gen. 29:30).

- God blessed Jacob by multiplying his profits (Gen. 30:27, 43).
- Jacob was irreplaceable to Laban, and his father-in-law fought to keep him in his employ (Gen. 30:28).

Showing you are reliable makes all the difference. If you say you'll do x by y, then prove you are dependable by meeting the expectation you set. Commit to keeping your promises, even if you don't use the word.

If you are reprimanded, don't make excuses—take responsibility. Simply listen without interruption and let your supervisor know you heard them. Show a willingness to dialogue until you clarify that you understand clearly what you can do to set things right. Assure them you will correct the situation according to their standards, and then do it.

What could Russ learn from Jacob? We can imagine a different outcome, if Russ followed the standards set by a man who lived thousands of years before him.

―⁓―

Russ stepped off the elevator and entered the glistening world of Leeholt Media Group. Julie called out a cheery, "Good morning."

Even though she sometimes got on his nerves, Russ made a pointed effort to think on her good points. She was the hub of communication for the entire building, after all. "How are you?"

"Great. Ready for a fabulous day."

"Hope so." Russ offered a faint smile in return for Julie's moon silver sparkle. He waved over his shoulder when he turned toward his office.

Russ sipped a cup of espresso while he waited for his computer to fire e-mail into his in-box. He sighed at Don's directive to pull the northwest sales stats before nine thirty.

Jerry poked his head in the door and interrupted Russ's thoughts. "Starting early, huh?"

"Got a lot to tackle."

"Have you heard if you got the promotion?"

Russ broke eye contact. "No."

"Did you ask about it?"

"Not yet. I'm planning to, though. I've been waiting for the right opportunity."

"It stinks when you have to remind your boss to keep his word. Maybe you should find another job."

"Maybe." Russ looked past Jerry and smiled faintly toward an unseen place. "I used to get myself worked up, convinced everyone else had it better than me, and then something I read changed my outlook. A single decision turned things around. I got my first raise within three months of practicing that resolve."

Jerry crossed the threshold and stepped deeper into the office. "Don't hold out on me. What'd you read?"

Russ blinked back to reality. "I got this idea from Jacob in the Bible."

Jerry walked to the chair across from Russ's desk and plopped down. "The Bible? You don't buy into that religious stuff, do you?"

"You might think it's silly, but the Bible has great ideas. Studying it made all the difference in my work habits, and the benefits speak for themselves."

"You're not saying your raises are the result of reading a book?"

"Not just any book, and not solely from reading it. You have to do something with what you read. Someone once said, 'When you stand before God, he won't ask you what you read but what did you do with what you read.'"

Leather squeaked under Jerry when he shifted in the chair. A brow of confusion wrinkled his forehead. "What's this got to do with making decisions that are going to get me raises?"

"Be careful. You can't make your motive about what you get. You read the Bible to soak up knowledge, so you can exercise discipline and apply what you learn. Then wisdom gives your words meaning."

Jerry stood up. "I still don't see how reading something written thousands of years ago could make a difference in my life."

Russ got up, walked to the front of his desk, and leaned against it. "Have you ever heard of Jacob?"

Jerry folded his arms. "Can't say I have."

"His example transformed my thinking. Here's a guy who was promised something he really wanted. Jacob agreed to work seven years so he could marry the woman he loved. But then his father-in-law, Laban, pulled a fast one. Because of the culture, Laban was able to trick Jacob into marrying his older daughter."

Jerry sat back down. "Are you kidding me?"

Russ laughed. "Anyway, Laban offered to also let Jacob marry Rachel if he worked another seven years."

"While he was still married to the first one?"

"Consider the times. But don't get distracted by cultural differences. The point is Jacob deeply wanted Rachel. So he agreed to the terms. He would work seven more years so he could live with the woman he loved. Now he's up to fourteen years of dedicated labor so he can have her."

Jerry propped his elbows on his knees and leaned forward. "No way."

"That's not even the amazing part of the story. Because of the customs in their day, after Jacob married Leah, they celebrated for an entire week."

"Who's Leah?"

"The older sister. The first wife." Russ sipped his espresso. "At the end of his wedding week with Leah, Laban goes ahead and lets Jacob marry Rachel, too. So now, he has what he really wanted all along, but he hadn't worked the additional seven years yet."

Jerry's eyes lit up. "I'd be out of there."

"Exactly, that's my point."

"What, to take the girl and run?"

"No. In today's world, most of us would do exactly what you said. If we got what we wanted, regardless of the promise we made, we'd split with the goods."

"Why not?"

"That's what I learned. Jacob's actions backed up his word. It set him apart. And God blessed all of his work because of it. Go look up the details. This guy eventually prospered even more than Laban, his former employer. All because he behaved with integrity. He didn't take the easy way, but it sure paid off in the end."

"That's a crazy story."

"One worth reading and emulating. I learned to change my everyday habits one sentence at a time, thanks to Jacob." Russ glanced at his watch. "And speaking of, I need to get back to work. Don wants me to have the sales stats from the northwest region to him by nine thirty. If I start now, I can turn them in ahead of schedule."

Jerry got back up and walked to the door. He hesitated and looked back at Russ, before stepping into the hallway. "The Bible. Who knew?"

Russ sat in front of his computer and grinned at Jerry. "I'd say God did."

Jerry drummed his fingers on the door frame and said, "Hmm," then he was gone.

True to his word, Russ finished the stats and e-mailed them ahead of the deadline. Later that afternoon, he got the chance to ask Don about the promotion.

His boss blanched white. "I'm really sorry, I've been meaning to talk with you. We gave the position to Jones."

Russ could feel his blood pressure drop.

"But," Don smiled, "we have a different position in mind for you. A better one. I've watched you grow over the past months, and we need a guy like you on the global team. I'd like to move you over as early as next week. If you're interested."

Stunned, Russ reached out to shake his boss's hand. "You bet."

Over the next few years, Russ's reputation grew. He received promotions and raises, until he eventually surpassed the goals he'd set for himself when he was first hired by Leeholt Media.

Ultimately, Russ started his own media company, and word spread that Russ was a man you could count on. Prestigious clients flocked for representation. Other companies, high schools, and colleges started asking him to teach seminars. Russ shared his secret to success. A story in the Bible about one man who did what he said, even after he got what he wanted.

———

Laban actually gave Jacob Rachel's hand in marriage directly after Leah's bridal week, BEFORE Jacob worked the extra seven years. This makes Jacob's integrity even more stunning, because in today's society, most of us would justify leaving with everything, or maybe just Rachel, since we were deceived. But who among us would have kept our word and worked the extra seven years AFTER we already received what we were working for? Especially when we discover we agreed to do the work under false pretenses on the part of our employer?

Becoming irreplaceable is a matter of keeping our word, and building a foundation of good patterns. Can we create patterns that will ensure positive results on a permanent basis? I believe we can, and we'll explore the possibilities in our next chapter.

———— Investigative Questions ————

1. Do you set an example of good speech, conduct, love, faith, and purity? (1 Tim. 4:12).

2. Do you know it's better not to make a vow than to make one and not fulfill it? (Eccles. 5:5).

3. Do you destroy your neighbors with your mouth, or does knowledge help you escape trouble? (Prov. 11:9).

PART TWO

Growth Principles

Chapter 5

The Paul Pattern

A meaningful life is a courageous life—
one built on facts, not illusion.

I've seen many people self-destruct. And yet, once the dust settles on the aftermath of their habits, they still can't figure out why a pattern of bad things keeps happening to them. Stuck, these folks get up and languish in the characteristics that caused them this hurt in the first place. They don't see their consequences as a natural result of cause and effect. Instead, they blame others for the outcomes of their behaviors.

This is not irreplaceable behavior.

But what causes someone to get on a hamster wheel of failure? Do people simply want to feel bad?

In my experience, I would answer a resounding NO. I'm not familiar with one human being who likes depression, a cloud of anger, anxiety, disillusionment, or the symptoms that accompany them. People want to live a meaningful life, and yet most don't know how to incorporate small changes that lead to big differences.

We rarely pay attention to where our minds roam. We don't realize our focus is on feeling good in a particular moment, instead of resolving to accept responsibility and change habits.

According to The Marlin Company – Workplace Communications Experts™, most employees don't realize how much power they have to influence success on the job. Their actions cost or contribute to everyone they work with. The Marlin Company's survey methodology targets hundreds of employees nationwide. Because of personal experience, I wholeheartedly agree with the published results of their 2010 survey.

Among the most serious issues these days—and the hardest to communicate—were a lack of positive attitudes and morale; a need for more employees to focus on responsibility and accountability for their own morale, as well as contributing to collective morale; and integrity, ethical behavior, and engagement in the workplace despite anxiety about the economy.

Other issues: respect for co-workers; concentration on the details; avoiding rumors and gossip; and taking the time to follow company procedures.

"People everywhere are still very distracted by economic anxiety," said Frank Kenna III, president of the Marlin Company. "Many are concerned about job loss, or reduced hours, or the loss of a job by a spouse. This takes a huge emotional, mental and physical toll, and what we're seeing is thousands of workers partially blinded to the task at hand at any given time, making mistakes, causing accidents and taking it out on co-workers in an insensitive and undiplomatic way. What also came through loud and clear was the critical need for managers and employees to communicate to assuage fears and improve morale."[2]

One of the great dangers in today's workplace is vain imaginations. Assuming others are thinking or saying things about us. Events reach a critical point when assumptions become accusations, either behind the back, or face-to-face. Instead of asking questions with an open mind, statements are made based on preconceived ideas of what the other thinks about us.

Doubts are raised, misplaced motives are presupposed—illusion becomes the viewer's truth. Emotions smother the facts. The world being out to get us becomes the dagger at the heart of our misinformed actions.

We jeopardize our own jobs when we believe others harbor ill motives.

Tom shows us how our emotions can convince us to pull away. Tom's outward focus blocks inner wisdom. The results speak for themselves.

—⁓—

Tom climbed the scaffold and teetered for balance on the beam holding his weight. He spit and watched the white sputum cloud disappear long before it hit the ground below.

He didn't notice the soft rustle in his brown hair or the purity of the air at this height. But laughter did catch his attention. He glanced angrily at Greg and Wally, on the next partition over, then turned back to his own piece of steel.

Tom clipped the edge of his welding mask with the butt of the rod and let it thunk over his face. The familiar blue-white crackle drowned his grumblings. He liked the familiar tendrils of smoke and the scorched scent they left in his nostrils. When he finished the first row, he shoved the mask up, and glared toward his co-workers again.

Steadied at each end of a shared beam, they made quick work of the steel in front of them. In between smoky arcs, echoes of their good-humored conversation floated like bird's wings across the open blue sky. His emotions inflamed even more.

Tom turned back to his task. "If I had help, I'd get done faster too. Jerks." He still had at least two hours of shoulder-throbbing work before he finished, and they were taking a break.

Over the past several months, some of the men had razzed Tom about Greg stealing his job as crew chief. Lately, it seemed their jabs were on target. Greg not only got the gravy jobs but help whenever he wanted. The more Tom felt his authority slip away, the more incensed he became.

A few minutes later, Tom watched the two men climb into the grated elevator. He glared at the High Point Construction sign screwed into the tram gate, until it lowered beyond his sight.

Tom groused while he scooted sideways toward the next piece of steel. "Greg's got Wally and the rest of the crew on his side. I knew he'd do anything to take my job. He's been after it for months."

Alone under a pulsing sun, Tom's emotions built until they snapped like his welds. By the time he made his way to the ground, over three hours later, he was in a dark mood. Mentally, he dared anyone to cross him. Tom was ripe for a meltdown.

Joe, the site boss, met him as the elevator gate creaked open. "Can you hop on the forklift and move those concrete forms to the west side of the building? Greg needs the room so he can assemble the wiring for our next phase."

"But I've always staged the wiring."

Joe clapped Tom's shoulder. "I've got a couple of other projects I'd like you to head up. Greg can handle the wiring."

"You're taking my job away."

Joe turned in the opposite direction and began to walk. "Don't be territorial," he said over his shoulder, "or paranoid."

Tom stewed for a few seconds before stomping toward the forklift. He plopped in the worn vinyl seat and cranked the key. A series of beeeep, beeeeep, beeeeeeps warned anyone in the vicinity that the machine was backing up.

Tom slammed the knob so the lift would change from reverse to a forward motion. The whole carriage jerked when he shifted. Movement to Tom's right caught his attention.

Greg grinned like a cartoon weasel while he readied full coils of black wiring for relocation. And wouldn't you know it? Wally was helping.

Tom gunned the forklift but didn't take his eyes off the other two men.

BAM.

The noise jolted him as much as the rocking of the entire machine. His head bounced off the cushioned bar running across the top of the lift. Tom cursed and cupped his head with his right hand. He gingerly cranked his neck forward to see what had caused him to come to a sudden stop. Tom groaned at the sight.

The crumpled grill on Joe's Ford work truck bore evidence of Tom's lapse in concentration. Within moments, a barrage of voices circled the forklift. They shouted questions and barked contrasting orders.

"Back up."

"Don't move."

"Are you okay?"

"Are you stupid?"

"What happened?"

"Why weren't you paying attention?"

Then Joe's controlled baritone quieted the harmony of conflict. "Tom, are you hurt?"

"I'm fine. Sorry, boss."

"Do you have any pain? Can you move your arms and legs?"

"I hit my head on the roll bar, but that's it."

Joe veed his eyebrows. "Go ahead and back up a few inches. Carefully."

Mangled metal screeched and scratched as the forklift hiccupped backwards. The left headlight on Joe's truck tumbled out of its socket and hung by threadlike wires. One of the gold plastic blinker covers slipped off the truck bumper and shattered on the ground.

"Hold up." Joe raised his hand. "Climb out. I'll have one of the guys clean up the debris and park the lift."

Tom eased from the carriage to stand in front of the carnage he'd caused.

Joe knelt to the ground and palmed a few shards of plastic. He let them siphon through his fingers, then brushed his hands and stood. He looked at Tom and squinted. "Walk with me."

Tom tried to ignore the ache climbing up the base of his skull as he fell in step beside his boss.

Joe walked toward the collision aftermath and motioned for Tom to follow. Joe ran his hand along the fender weld of his Ford. A piece of chrome molding caught the pocket of his pants. Joe swore and tugged the metal loose. "Where's your head at?"

Tom didn't dare confess the true reason for his lost focus. He scrambled for a feasible excuse. "I think my foot slipped off the brake and hit the accelerator. It happened pretty fast."

"I mean your distraction."

Caught off guard, Tom stopped walking. "I don't understand."

"Don't act like this is the first time I've discussed the subject with you. We've talked about your paranoia before."

Tom bristled, "I'm not paranoid. I've just got a lot on my mind. I heard Greg's after my job."

"Did you ask him about it?"

"No."

"Then I don't think you can make that statement."

"He wouldn't tell me the truth."

"How do you know if you don't make the effort to discuss it?"

"He can come to me."

"That's the attitude I'm concerned about."

Sensing peril, Tom formed his answer with slow apprehension. "I'll work on it, boss."

"I expect more from you, Tom."

"Got it." Tom motioned toward the hive of bodies buzzing around the wreckage. "Would you like me to help?"

Joe's words sighed from his diaphragm. "Just put your tools away. We need to fill out an accident report and have a doctor check you over."

"But I'm fine."

"Gotta follow procedure. After that, you can go home and get some rest. Unless the doctor says otherwise, I'll see you here in the morning."

Joe made Tom an appointment with the company doctor before filling out the paperwork on the accident. The atmosphere in the office trailer bristled with awkwardness. When they finished, Tom wiped sweat from his brow, though the air conditioner kept the tiny room cool.

Tom checked out fine and, once dismissed by the physician, sulked all the way home.

When one of his co-workers called to see how he felt, Tom interrogated him to see whether Joe had talked about him. Repeatedly, he was assured that nothing had been mentioned, but Tom didn't believe him. They all stuck up for each other.

By the next morning, when he arrived on the job site, Tom was convinced Greg and his cronies had developed a conspiracy. Even those who pretended to like him were just acting. He decided to call them out before the day was over.

Lost in his mental tirade, Tom didn't see Wally approach. The brush against his arm made Tom jump.

"Feeling better?" Wally smiled.

"Why? Hoping I don't?"

Wally flinched. "Of course not." Wally cleared his throat. "Where did that come from?"

"You don't fool me."

"Man, you've got some kind of problem. I just wanted to make sure you were okay."

"Go talk to your brown-nose buddies." Tom walked away, leaving Wally with a gaping mouth frozen in place.

By midmorning, Tom was working in a solitary corner on the ground level, directed by Joe to squeeze insulation between two-by-fours. According to Tom's standards, this menial task was a slap in the face. He ignored the mandatory safety glasses and face masks supplied by High Point Construction for all its workers.

When he came to a bundle of wires hanging near the door frame, Tom laid the blower on the plywood floor. Joe had explicitly said to leave the electrical work to Greg, but Joe was brainwashed. If Tom could show how much better he was, then Joe would appreciate the value of a good man's work.

Tom imagined an apologetic Joe while he deftly cut, spliced, and twisted wires.

Trying to hurry, Tom flew through the mangled mess. He wanted to finish before Joe rerouted him back to the job he was supposed to be working on. Besides, he needed to prove he was fast as well as thorough, so he sped up, anticipating the pleasant surprise on Joe's face.

Zap. A jolt knocked Tom fifteen feet backwards.

He blinked several times, trying to shake the fog in his brain. It took a couple of minutes for his blurred vision to clear. A buzzing sound swarmed his ears. The smell of burnt hair haloed around his forehead. He felt something warm across his arm, but when he looked, instead of a soft piece of cotton, he saw red blood pumping across a deep gash. A splintered plank appeared to be the weapon.

Tom tried to yell, but the only sound his vocal chords released was a sharp rasp. He gathered spittle in his mouth and swallowed, then tried again. "Help." It was weak, but at least a word formed. He wet his throat and made another attempt, stronger this time. "Help."

Footsteps. Tom let his head fall back on the plywood in relief. A darkening ooze began to spread across his brain. The last words he heard were Joe's.

"Man, you've really done it this time."

Then everything blinked black.

———

Tom made the mistake of many employees in today's work world. He assumed a great deal, and disregarded his employer's specific directive. He paid a costly price. Most on-the-job accidents are caused by broken concentration. Most mistakes are the result of inattention to detail. Worst cases can cost employees their life. Some cases cost them their job. Best cases cost raises and promotions.

When we don't pay attention to our thoughts, we pay. And the expense of negative thinking isn't just ours to bear. The people around us often suffer consequences, too.

This is one reason dealing with our problems honestly and head-on matters. Instead of simmering in perceived wrongs, the wise person goes to the source of conflict. Instead of standing our ground and making accusations, we can take a humble stance and ask questions to clarify, so we move closer to true resolution.

We would do well to distinguish the facts so we can wisely decide when to submit and when to stand. Emotional decisions usually mislead us into foolish actions. Paul's life, as documented in the Bible, provides a solid example of a man who changed his patterns for the better.

- The first time we meet Paul, he's going by his birth name, Saul. He's thriving on the emotional hype of the crowd around him—to the point of approving the death of an innocent young man. Paul's goal in life appears to be the destruction of people and possessions for his own selfish gain. He believes he's motivated by the right things (Acts 7:57–60; 8:1–3).
- When Saul was reprimanded, he fell to the ground (Acts 9:3–4).
- Saul learned from his humiliation and obeyed down to the smallest detail when directed to get up and take action (Acts 9:8–9).
- Saul took the time to regain his strength before moving ahead (Acts 9:19).
- Immediately, Saul spoke boldly, not allowing fear to hinder him from proclaiming the message of truth (Acts 9:20–22).
- Saul investigated the facts and acted wisely based on the information (Acts 9:23–25).

- Saul, who was now called Paul, did not trust his own instincts about the inclinations of others. He stopped throwing stones and leaned on the Holy Spirit of God to show him the motives of other men (Acts 13:9–12).

The willingness of Paul to trust God rather than his own feelings gave him the ability to separate fact from emotion. Though his life was far from perfect, his decision to follow the true source of wisdom gave him a clear conscience and kept him focused on a meaningful life.

Sometimes we are fast to jump to conclusions at work. But a onetime occurrence does not point to intentional wrongdoing. We can look for patterns of behavior to help us identify true intent. Even in ourselves.

The world today shouts that we should follow our own path. Our truth is the only correct truth for us. If you feel it, it must be right. But these self-serving attitudes fail us at work.

Imagine an employer telling a subordinate to do a particular job.

If the employee says, "I won't do what you told me; I must follow my own truth and do things my way. Your truth isn't my truth," do you think that employee would have a job very long?

Most states allow for firing based on insubordination with no repercussions to the employer. And they should.

Hierarchy exists because it keeps order. Authority figures usually have their jobs because they earned them. If not, except in uncommon situations, they won't hold the position for long. Cause and effect will ultimately have their way.

When my children were young, I taught them about choice and consequence. If you choose to pick up a stick lying on the ground, the other end automatically rises, too. So our consequences rise with the choices we make—in unison. If you pick up a choice, you automatically pick up a consequence, the other end of the stick.

Over a period of time, our choices become patterns. And so do our consequences.

Tom initially made his decisions based on emotional misunderstandings. Could Tom move from irrational to irreplaceable? Let's see what happens when he changes his pattern to ask more questions and makes fewer statements based on preconceptions. How might this choice affect his outcome?

———

The breeze blew briskly at the seventh-story elevation where Tom swung on a scaffold. He'd been with High Point Construction for nearly twelve years and worked his way to crew chief on their larger projects. But lately, rumors made it sound as if his position was in jeopardy.

With the slump in the housing market and commercial construction at all-time lows, Tom worried about the welfare of his wife and kids. Bonuses were already a thing of the past, health insurance costs were rising, and putting food on the table was tougher than ever. If he lost his crew chief pay, he might not make the mortgage for more than a couple of months. Tom's family counted on the extra money.

"If you don't quit daydreaming, you'll be up here all night." Greg's laughter melded with Wally's, while the two men teamworked their welding efforts a few feet over.

"Glad I could amuse you."

The fact that Greg was the source of the ribbing caused Tom to fret even more.

An hour after Greg and Wally took the elevator down, Tom did the same. He only had one foot out when the hoots started.

"Get lost?"

"Running behind, old man?" Greg's voice rang with glee.

Tom smiled and shook his head in response to their barbs. He hoped his nonchalant act was convincing. He checked his watch. Tom planned to spend his lunch break reflecting.

Before he made it to the time clock, Joe stopped him. "After lunch, could you move those forms so Greg can stage the wiring?"

Alarm welled in Tom's chest. "You don't want me to do it?"

"I've got a couple of other projects in mind for you." Joe slapped Tom between the shoulder blades. "Go ahead and take lunch, then you can move the forms."

"Yes, sir." Tom headed to his truck. After he climbed into the vehicle, an unseen wind tossed a discarded newspaper across the windshield. He glimpsed the headline, "Economists Argue: Rebound or Recession?"

Tom opened his lunch box and took a bite of roast beef and cheese. He savored the bite of horseradish while picking up the worn, black book on the seat beside him. He was reading through the Bible, and this morning had gotten to chapter 7 in the book of Acts. A new story was developing—Saul had come into the picture.

Over the next forty-five minutes, Tom studied the transformation of Saul to Paul. He noted how Saul asked questions and bowed before Jesus on the road to Damascus. He jotted a few bullet points in a small black journal.

- Change in name—who does God say you are?
- Change in appearance—do you look like Jesus?
- Change in outlook—based on facts.
- Change to trust—Christ provides for all our needs.

When lunch ended, Tom prayed before he clocked back in with fresh determination. The tonnage on his back was gone. He'd decided to let God handle the economy and concentrate on doing what was within his power to affect.

Tom focused the forklift's movements. In short order, he had the forms cleared, providing a clear path for the staging project.

"Thanks old man," Greg grinned, as Tom got out of the forklift.

"Have you got a minute?" Tom said.

"What's on your mind?"

Tom squared himself to face his co-worker. "I wanted to bring a concern straight to the source."

"Yeah?"

"Rumor is, you're after my job."

"Don't blame me because the guys are talking."

"Hear me out. I'm not accusing you of anything. But I did want to ask. What are your intentions?"

Greg's face turned rosy. He seemed to have trouble getting the words out of his mouth. When they finally came, there was a croak in his voice. "Look man, I'm trying to get by like everyone else. Don't come crying to me if Joe wants someone younger for the job."

"Is that what he said?"

"Nah, but scuttlebutt is scuttlebutt."

"I see. I just want you to know there are no hard feelings. If you need help with anything, let me know. Some of that wiring can get tricky, and I'd be glad to give you a hand."

Greg was still frozen in place when Tom left to find Joe.

His boss was fumbling with the insulation blower when Tom arrived. "Need help?"

Joe's pinched features relaxed at Tom's offer. "Perfect timing."

"Can we talk while we work?"

"What's on your mind?"

Tom hoisted a bag of insulation off the floor. "I heard some of the guys talking."

Joe pulled the hatch on the blower open so Tom could pour the contents of his bag in it. "Oh?"

"It seems most of the crew thinks you're priming Greg to take my job as chief." The last remnants of insulation trickled into the blower, and Tom laid the bag on the floor.

Joe closed the hatch and reclined against a pile of lumber. One arm crossed his chest and supported his elbow, allowing his left hand to clutch his cocked chin. "I admit I considered it." He scratched the side of his head. "Greg brought a few things to my attention. Areas of untapped potential we haven't made use of."

Tom inhaled into his lower diaphragm. "I understand, boss. I won't try to talk you out of any decision you make. God will take care of me and my family, but I do ask you to consider my qualifications. Don't get me wrong, Greg's a great fellow with lots of talent."

"Yes, he is."

"I only want to remind you of my years of experience and loyalty to the company. I'm dedicated to doing a good job. But I'll honor whatever choices you make. And I'll support whomever you put in a position of leadership."

Joe leaned forward. "I admit, your attitude surprises me. I would have expected a different reaction. Wish I had a few more around here who thought like you do. Thanks for coming to talk to me about this. I'll take it into consideration."

Over the next few months, Tom stopped listening to the gossip and focused on following company procedures. As weeks of consistent behavior change continued, Greg became increasingly irritated at Tom's pattern of calm demeanor.

Their roles reversed. Greg lashed out of his emotions, while Tom steadied his actions on facts. Greg's sniping only made Tom stand out more.

Joe noticed. Tom kept his job as crew chief and soon earned a rare raise to boot. Like Paul, Tom's patterns of behavior changed, and when he picked up new choices, new consequences and opportunities rose along with them.

Irreplaceable employees don't allow seeds of doubt, assumptions, or vain imaginations to make illusion appear as truth. In the Bible, we are encouraged to go directly to the source and separate fact from emotion. With correct information, to the best of our ability, we can live at peace or shake the dust off each situation. Every choice brings a consequence into our lives and the lives of those we care for.

Paul dropped his stones, and we should in the workplace. Stop assuming we know better, work better, deserve better than our fellow employees.

Don't allow resentment and bitterness to steal your blessings.

Heroic actions often bring stellar results and can surprise those around us. Heroes don't join the crowd.

The world can't help noticing a change in pattern that sets us apart from others. As long as we don't let fear get in the way. In the pages ahead, we'll learn how to avoid the paralyzing clutch of this wily enemy.

——————Investigative Questions ——————

1. Are you thankful? Or do you allow vain imaginations to make you foolish and darken your heart? (Rom. 1:21).

2. Do you submit to God, and are you at peace with him, so that prosperity will come to you? (Job 22:21).

3. Are you conformed to the pattern of this world? Or continually transformed by the renewing of your mind, so that you can test and approve God's good, pleasing, and perfect will? (Rom. 12:2).

Chapter 6

The Esther Endeavor

In order to succeed, we must trust
our faith more than our fears.

Fear can keep us from becoming irreplaceable. It holds more power than any other emotion to drive us to wave the white flag of surrender. Like a dog captivated by its own tail, fear wiggles in front of our eyes, and we chase it in circles. God's best is replaced with could-be, might-happen, and what-if. "What if" exemplifies a what-I-fear question. Yet, most of what we fear never happens.

The Bible says fear of the Lord is the beginning of wisdom, so we can add the corollary: fear of anything else generates foolishness. How many people shuffle through life, afraid to risk, expecting abstract possibilities of the worst? Doomsday thinking and chronic complaints deceive minds and alter reactions. Energy is consumed by imagination and cannot be used for positive action. Candice is a prime example of someone imprisoned by fear.

Candice married Grant Denton right after college graduation. His 5' 8" was a nice balance to her 5' 6". She spotted his smooth blond hair, almond-shaped green eyes, and studious demeanor in their New Testament Studies class. Though her shy nature never allowed her to show obvious interest, they locked eyes a couple of times when she tried to sneak a glance his direction.

When he asked her for a lunch date, Candice's tied tongue wouldn't let her speak, so she offered a nod for an answer. He coaxed a time out of her, and everything was set.

When the day arrived, he took her on a leisurely afternoon walk through the park. Soon enough, Grant's easy dialogue stirred a confident flow of banter from Candice. They held similar beliefs, backgrounds, and interests. Both solidly stated a commitment to Christian living.

Midway through their stroll, the atmosphere changed. Grant told Candice about his mom's struggle with cancer during his teens. "The chemo was brutal. Every morning I wondered whether it would be a good day or a bad one. Sometimes I'd hide in my room, because it made me mad to see her suffer. After all these years, I still panic when she has a doctor's appointment. You never know when it will come back. I don't take anything for granted now."

Candice stopped in her tracks. She looked up at him through sheepish eyes. Her voice cracked with emotion. "I lost my mom to cancer when I was fifteen. She was diagnosed right before my fourteenth birthday."

Grant gently pushed dark bangs off her pale forehead. "I'm so sorry." He guided her into his arms and let her shed quiet tears into his shirt.

A few minutes later, she pulled away in apology. "I'm sorry, I never do this."

"Shh, I understand," he said. And she knew he did.

From that day on, Candice and Grant were together every moment time allowed. And marriage soon followed. They spent late nights dreaming of faraway, exotic missionary trips, changing lives, and discovering worlds they'd only heard about.

They spent their money frugally and looked for jobs in ministry. His passion drove him to an interest in young married couples, while she wanted to work with children. They prayed with determination to find the jobs meant exclusively for them.

Then one evening something happened. Candice finished cleaning the kitchen and settled in to watch television. Grant cruised the Internet. "Honey, you've got to see this," he shouted.

"Can't I look at it later?" Candice grouched.

"No. Honey, this is huge."

"All right, I'm coming." She stood over his shoulder, and her face lit up when she looked at the screen. "Wow."

Grant beamed, "This is what we've been praying for. The church is small, it's in the northwest, and they need an associate pastor. They specifically want to build a young couples ministry. My theology focus makes it a perfect fit."

"Let's apply," she said. They spent the next two hours pouring their lives into the computer profile. When they finally went to bed, Candice found she went from groggy to an adrenaline boost, and now sleep was impossible. Her thoughts whirled in excitement. All their dreams really could come true.

After seven excruciating weeks, Candice and Grant's wait ended. Grant opened his e-mail after work and discovered a reply from Crossroads Community Church.

Dear Mr. & Mrs. Denton:

On behalf of Crossroads Community Church, we would like to extend our invitation for an interview regarding your recent application. Your qualifications appear particularly suited for our needs, and we would like the opportunity to meet you. We will prayerfully make a decision based on your response and our time together.

Sincerely,
Eric Chambers
Pastoral Search Committee Chair

Grant and Candice floated through the interview process and nailed the job. The salary package was modest, even for a pair of young newlyweds, but it came with a tiny parsonage. The generosity of congregant hearts would subsidize any shortfalls, and besides, they could live on love.

Sixteen years, five moves, three daughters, two dogs, four hospitalizations, and many childhood diseases later, the Dentons landed in the southwest. Grant was satisfied with yet another low-paying, small-church ministry job, and once again Candice worked hard to fill the financial gaps.

Every time she tried to talk to Grant about money, she felt like he blew her off. "God will provide," he'd say.

Candice silently grumbled. Well, God helps those who help themselves, doesn't he? Grant's supposed to be the head of the household. He expects me to plan the budget, pay the bills, buy the food, take care of the house, and pull money out of thin air. My job at the Sonshine Christian School doesn't cover all that.

Times were tough. The car was on the fritz again, the bills came in faster than their paychecks, and college tuition loomed in the future. Candice prayed fervently just to get by.

It was another ordinary day in a succession of sameness that drove Candice to the brink. She stumbled out of bed to the clanging alarm clock. Her head pounded, and she tripped over a pile of clothes cluttering the floor. She said a quick prayer while she stepped in the shower. "Lord, please help me get out of this mess. I'm sick and tired of being sick and tired. Amen."

She got dressed, made coffee, woke the girls, and sipped the eye-opening brew while her children ate cold cereal. Once the dishes were piled on top of last night's in the sink, she trudged to the bedroom where Grant slept peacefully. Just looking at him made her mad.

It wasn't fair. She had to rush around, take care of the house, and make it to work on time. He got paid the same, no matter when he rolled out of bed. Sure, when he got up, he stayed busy, but he could do it on his schedule, not someone else's. And he got to do what he really loved, while she was stuck in a job she didn't necessarily hate, but definitely didn't like.

Candice left the house, stopped at the post office, and went to work at the school. She settled in with a sigh. Here, she hoped to escape overdue credit card statements, bank overdrafts, and three daughters who constantly nagged to keep up with their peers and the Disney Channel.

Mrs. Pierce, the school principal and head administrator, walked in and eyed the stack of mail. "Hi Candice, how are you this fine morning?"

"I'm good, thank you, just starting on the mail."

"You are such a blessing, my dear, thank you," Mrs. Pierce said as she left the envelopes to Candice. "I'll be on hall checks if you need me."

"Okay," Candice answered with a gentle smile. Mrs. Pierce walked out the door, and Candice worked the envelope flaps.

When she opened the third piece down, the words on the page caused her heart to beat a bit faster. Candice immediately started arguing with herself. Her thoughts riddled like bullets.

"I can't do it.

"But I just need a little help to get me out of this jam. Maybe God sent this in answer to my prayers.

"You know God doesn't send something wrong to make something right. You'll get caught!

"I could pay it off with our income tax refund before anyone ever knew.

"What if Grant found out? He'd kill you.

"He'll never find out. Besides, this could help me pay off my two small cards. Grant might leave me if he knew I forged his name to open those accounts.

"Just because you can, doesn't mean you should.

"And just because I'm scared, doesn't mean I'm bad."

Candice fingered the credit card offer. It was in the school's name, but she had access to all the right information. She got up from her chair, opened the door, and looked up and down the hall. The coast was clear. She closed the door, then sat down and deftly completed the form. She signed Mrs. Pierce's name and sealed the credit application in the postage-free envelope provided.

A ball of guilt tried to swell in her belly, but she pushed it away.

"I don't think Mrs. Pierce truly appreciates how much work I do. I don't complain, even when she has me do some of her work. I should get paid more. I'll bet no one else at this school struggles as much as me. It isn't fair. The harder I try, it seems the worse things get. I'm not asking for much, but I think I deserve a little relief. It isn't like I'm robbing a bank or holding someone up at gunpoint. I'll pay back every penny."

Her thoughts were interrupted by a knock on the door. Alice Revelle, one of the elementary teachers and a confidante, stepped in. "Hey, Candice, what's up?"

Candice discreetly swept the envelope into her purse and pasted a quiet smile on her face. "I'm just sifting through the mail."

"Doing part of Mrs. Pierce's job again?"

"I don't mind really. It isn't as bad as cleaning the lounge. I want to scream every time I walk in there. It amazes me that a group of grown adults behave worse than children. Why can't they throw away their own trash and clean their own coffee cups? I'm not a slave, although sometimes I'm treated like one."

"I know, Candice, it isn't fair. But I can assure you, I make sure I clean up before I leave the lounge."

"I know you do, Alice. It isn't you I'm worried about."

"Well, that's because you're a giver. You sacrifice more than anyone I know. Every time you tell me something else you've done, I shake my head in wonder."

"It's my Christian duty."

"Well, it's high time some of the other so-called Christians around here fulfilled their duty."

"Don't I know it," Candice countered.

"I'd better get back to my class. I just stopped to make a copy of my lesson plan for the substitute tomorrow."

"Okay, but hey, don't say anything about our talk. I don't want Mrs. Pierce or some of the other teachers getting mad at me. They'll make my life miserable if they find out how I really feel."

"No problem," Alice said.

It would be several months before the deception erupted. Candice juggled payments in the meantime.

Around the time each school credit card statement came due, she left the house early to beat Mrs. Pierce to the post office. Candice felt especially guilty when the principal gushed about her dedication and initiative.

Each day she rushed home at lunch, and at the end of her workday, to make sure she beat Grant to the mailbox. If he were to discover any one of the accounts she had secretly opened, her marriage might be over. He didn't erupt in anger often, but when he did, it was explosive. If he knew how much debt his name was penned to, things would get ugly.

At income tax time, she expected to pay the secret cards off with their refund. But life threw her in a tailspin when they only received part of the refund she expected.

In desperation, she tried to talk to their pastor in confidence. Of course, she didn't tell him everything but hinted at the slight financial difficulty she and Grant faced. He offered to pray with her and spouted a few Scriptures.

He mentioned things like strife, jealousy, outbursts of anger, and disputes. He couldn't think any of that applied to her. Candice always made sure she was the picture of grace.

If she wanted a sermon, she could wait for Sunday morning. He didn't care about her problems, nor did he try to. What she needed was someone to save her from the fear that kept her awake at night. Her pounding anxiety threatened to drive her to a nervous breakdown.

This chronic mind-set consumed her. She found herself snapping at people, especially her family and co-workers at school. Well, they were just going to have to deal with it. If they were under her pressure, they'd snap, too.

Then, on a beautiful autumn Thursday, Mrs. Pierce entered the secretary's office of the Sonshine Christian School. Outside, golden threads streamed around the mesa and flooded the room with an ethereal glow.

"Candice, we need to talk."

Something in Mrs. Pierce's tone signaled trouble. With a palpitating heart and clammy ice in her chest, Candice straightened and focused attention on her employer.

"I just received a phone call from a credit card company. This school doesn't operate off debt, so I was certain it was a mistake. This fax, however, says different. Isn't this your handwriting?"

Candice shifted uneasily and felt the color creep up her face. She didn't have to look to know what the page contained. Like a wounded animal, she felt the trap tighten around her limbs. Her back stiffened and she rose purposefully from the chair. Panic made her verbal attack swift and powerful. Mrs. Pierce could not have prepared for the onslaught.

Candice's words shot from her mouth. "It's not my fault. I planned to pay it back. No one ever listens to me. Most of the time, I'm treated like I'm invisible. It isn't fair, I try so hard, but everything goes wrong. Other people get all the breaks, why can't I get some? I do all the right things: I pray, I'm nice to people, I don't show my anger, and I never demand what I want. You tell me, how would you feel?"

"But Candice, we . . ."

Candice interrupted. "Don't start preaching at me. You don't know what it's like. You can't understand."

In a final, dramatic motion, she collapsed back into her chair. She could hear the chains clink as she imagined being thrown into debtor's prison. Tears streamed down her face while she waited for the authorities. Everything she'd fought to save was lost.

Candice allowed fear to drive her other emotions. By trying to ignore its existence, she fed its ravenous hunger for more of her life.

Defensiveness, entitlement, justification, and bitterness had come to rule. Sadly, Candice thought she masked them well.

But her hidden truth revealed a fear much deeper than her faith.

———

Not everyone in the workplace chooses a sin like Candice's. But please don't be deceived. Avoidance of excessive alcohol, sexual sin, or blatant theft does not necessarily protect you from job-threatening mistakes.

Candice's story demonstrates how fear seeds disgruntlement with potential for catastrophic outcomes. The power of fear dominated her life.

Most anger is driven by fear. Think about it: When was the last time you were angry? If you peel away the layers, is fear hiding in the center? Are you afraid there won't be enough money to pay the bills? Are you afraid no one notices your efforts? Are you afraid someone else gets more than you?

Fear in the workplace can drive us to justification—reprimand, job loss, or legal action may follow shortly after. All of us are one decision away from a life-altering event.

As humans, we must battle fear, but, for Christians, we have hope in the power of Jesus Christ. Repeatedly in his word, God reminds us in one form or another to "take courage and fear not."

The fiction of fear cannot compete with the fact of freedom. A mind-set of crippling fear allowed to thrive deceives us into chronic complaints and doomsday thinking. Christian courage sets us free.

Whether you believe in sovereign origin or not, it's hard to deny there are definitive answers to today's problems in the Bible. Esther 4:1–17 provides a courageous example for the problem of fear. When faced with a choice between death and life, she dared to take courage. She chose the high road, and the position God placed her in made her irreplaceable.

Let's peek into the heart of a woman who started out in fear but ultimately risked death to fulfill a purpose greater than her own life.

- Esther gathered her facts before taking action (Esther 4:5).
- Though terrified, Esther stated honestly what she was afraid of and why. She did not ignore the situation or pretend things were different than they were (Esther 4:10–12).
- Once resolved to the truth of Mordecai's words, Esther fasted and prayed and recruited others for support before making a move. With determination, she prepared herself to act on the behalf of others, even if it meant losing her own life (Esther 4:15–17).
- At the end of her fast, Esther kept her word and entered the place of her greatest fear. She steeled herself to die if necessary to do the right thing (Esther 5:1–3).
- Esther didn't reveal everything at the onset. She wisely used intrigue in her favor. She allowed human curiosity to help draw the king's interest to her request (Esther 5:4–8).
- Instead of trying to invoke her own retribution to enemies, she allowed them to fall into their own consequences, based on their pattern of poor behaviors (Esther 7:7–8).

Esther feared, but she ultimately took courage in choosing God's way. She agreed with Mordecai on a fact-based plan and kept her promises. As a result, the Jews were saved because Esther made the brave decision to trust God more than her fears. She was given the job of queen for just that moment in history.

How does this relate to you?

How do you know you weren't placed in your position for such a time as this? Is it possible your work offers a place for courage, a time of purpose, and an opportunity for heroics? Each day could prepare you for a future event, intended for an historical moment later.

If you are out of work, have you fasted and prayed? Have you separated facts from emotions to get a clear reading on the next steps you should take? Have you kept your promises and followed up with appropriate action? Do you trust God more than your fears?

Following Esther's example might have meant a different outcome for Candice.

They were barely moved into their parsonage at Crossroads Community Church when Grant and Candice received the news. There would be no health insurance.

"We can't afford a baby right now," Candice wailed.

"It won't do any good to fret." Grant stroked her arms. "God will provide."

Feeling put in her place, Candice choked back a wisp of fear. The claustrophobic emotion would grow over the coming months, fed by hormones and rising medical bills.

Candice fought memories of the financial toll her mother's cancer had wreaked on their family. Images of a near-empty refrigerator, watching her dad cry when he read the contents of another envelope stamped past due, the embarrassment of unfashionable clothes.

This was not the life she wanted as an adult or the life she wanted for her child. And yet, she didn't dare speak. She stuffed her fear deep into dark crevices. Places she didn't even allow God.

The day Abby arrived, all squiggly pink toes and soft baby smell, Candice allowed hope to shine on her darkness. For a little while.

But only a few weeks later, with dirty diapers festering in the trash and baby squalls piercing her peace, Candice fell apart. The past-due medical bill melted her into an emotional puddle.

When Grant walked in the door, she blubbered while he listened. After she vented and they discussed the options, they came to one practical conclusion—as much as neither one of them liked it, Candice needed to get a job.

With their contacts in the church, Candice landed a full-time position at a local day care. Abby went with her, Candice loved working with the kids, and the site was close to home. They chipped away at the bills and, after a few months, felt like they could breathe again.

A medical plan was soon added to Grant's salary package. So when Candice became pregnant again, they celebrated instead of worrying.

But shortly after Leah was born, things changed, and once again Candice felt like the rug was ripped from underneath her life. Without consulting her, Grant accepted a new position at a church up north. The pay and benefits were somewhat better, but Candice hated the thought of leaving stability behind.

They said sad good-byes, packed the family belongings into their Volkswagen, and put six hundred miles between them and their first home. Candice grieved silently but smiled outwardly. She couldn't let her husband down.

The first sign of trouble came within twenty-four hours. They rushed Abby to the hospital, lethargic and pale. It took four days for the doctors to break her spiked fever with medication. Almost a week and thousands of dollars later, Abby came home. Grant hadn't been on the job long enough for health insurance to cover the expenses.

Candice tried not to panic and found a job as a secretary to an insurance agent. She worked hard, while silent resentments grew. Weeks turned into months. Candice developed a pattern of burying fear and pretending everything was okay.

Time passed quickly. Before she knew it, sixteen years, five moves, three daughters, two dogs, four hospitalizations, and many childhood diseases came and went. And then the Dentons landed in the southwest, where Grant took another mediocre-paying, small-church ministry job. Once again, Candice worked hard to fill the financial gaps.

She struggled but managed to keep up with the bills while working as secretary at the Sonshine Christian School. Temptation reared its attractive head in the form of a credit card offer made out to her and Grant. This was not the first. Possibilities rampaged while she crumpled the enrollment form in her hands. Maybe this time financial relief was at her fingertips.

Candice let the piece of paper flutter to the tabletop and bowed her head. "Dear God, you know how tough things are. I feel boxed in, like there's no way out. Please protect me from myself and keep me from temptation. Don't let me do this again."

She opened her Bible and read a few sentences. Then, a single thought flitted across her mind. Go see Pastor Scott.

It felt like someone was choking the air from her esophagus as Candice knocked on the door. He was expecting her, but she dreaded explaining why she made the appointment. This man was more than her pastor: he was her husband's superior at work.

Once she got started, spilling a few details came easier than Candice expected, though she didn't tell him everything. She flinched when Pastor Scott asked personal questions about their spending habits. His Scripture offerings in response to her answers made her squirm in the wing-backed chair across from his desk.

Candice couldn't keep the whining from her voice when asked about her job.

Pastor Scott leaned forward and, though he sounded compassionate, his tone equally expressed firm intention in what he said. "If I might suggest, go home and read Esther with fresh eyes. It's one of the shorter books in the Bible. When you read it, ask God to show you if there's anything you can apply to your work."

Candice thanked him for his time and left the office. She muttered to herself on the way to the car, "That was a waste. I didn't even tell him about the card."

A silent voice answered in her head. "It can't hurt to try Pastor Scott's idea. What's the worst that will happen? You'll be where you are right now."

Candice shrugged and answered the voice. "I guess it can't hurt." She drove straight home and opened the book of Esther.

After reading through the story once, Candice grabbed a notebook and pen and then jotted down particular points that seemed applicable to her own situation. Reviewing the list made something she'd missed suddenly visible.

She could see how fear fueled the seething anger she tried to hide from the world. Driven by her past, Candice was afraid financial ruin would force her children to endure some of the hardships she had after her mother died.

But instead of voicing her concerns to Grant, Candice hoped they'd simply go away. And she'd helped make things worse by not having the courage to speak up.

Candice asked God to forgive her and provide the strength to confess the secret credit card account to Grant. The one she'd opened a few months earlier. And then, she committed to fast and pray for three days.

At the end of the third day, Candice thought about Esther's terror when approaching the king. Candice thought she could relate as she dressed up and approached her husband. Grant might not have a golden scepter, but he could place her head on an emotional chopping block.

Twice, Candice almost caved and ran away. But finally, with intention, she drew a deep breath and risked her husband's wrath.

He looked up and his eyes lit. "Wow, what's the occasion? I haven't seen you this dolled up in a long time."

Fat tears instantly balled under her lashes and rolled off her chin. She knelt beside his chair.

Concern splashed across his face, Grant leaned forward and stroked Candice's hair. "Honey, what's wrong?"

Candice shook her head side to side and thought sadly that it might be easier if she were sick. "I need to tell you something. Please hear me out, and try not to interrupt. Just let me finish before you say anything."

"Of course." Grant's brows wrinkled together.

Candice looked at the floor. "I've done something terrible." She could hear a whistling noise as Grant took a sharp breath and held. But he didn't speak.

She dared a peek under her lashes to view Grant's pale face. "Without your knowledge, I opened a credit card account . . ."

"You did what?" his voice boomed with explosive anger.

"Please, you promised to let me finish."

"I didn't know you were going to drop a bomb like this."

"It sort of happened. I didn't mean to. But money was so tight, and the offer came in the mail. It was all too easy. I sign your paychecks when I make deposits, so I just signed the credit application."

Grant jumped out of his chair. "You signed my name. As if it isn't bad enough—you put my name to your deception." He marched for the front door.

Sobbing, Candice pleaded, "Where are you going? I'm sorry. I'm so sorry."

"Those papers didn't crawl into your hands and force your fingers to sign my name. This didn't just happen. I need to clear my head." He placed his hand around the doorknob.

"Are you coming back?"

"I don't know what I'm going to do." And with that, the door slammed.

Grant returned several hours later, but anger broiled in the home for weeks. Pastor Scott suggested a Christian marriage counselor who specialized in money matters. The church covered two months of basic expenses so they could regain their footing.

They pecked away at the bills and learned how to deal with their buried emotions. Candice grew stronger in voicing things directly, honestly, and yet gently with her family, boss, and co-workers. She was surprised to find people often reacted positively to her requests. She also discovered most of them didn't automatically know what she wanted and weren't trying to keep her from her desires.

And then one day, temptation reared its pretty head. Candice opened the morning mail at the school. Though she and Grant were knocking down their debt, they were a long way off from a clean slate. The easy offer in her hand sure would help.

Candice scanned the credit card invitation, gulped, and pulled the Esther notes from her purse. A quick review and prayer prepared her for what she needed to do.

Candice went on the hunt for the school administrator. Sitting in Mrs. Pierce's office, she confessed the temptation. Candice half expected to get fired.

But Mrs. Pierce surprised her. "What you told me took a great deal of courage. I appreciate your honesty. The fact that you didn't hide your temptation says a lot about your character. I hope you always feel comfortable talking to me."

Candice could feel her mouth open involuntarily.

Mrs. Pierce reached down and unlocked a desk drawer. She pulled out a leather-bound binder. When she flipped it open, she scrawled across a page. Then she tore out the page and offered it to Candice. "I've watched your attitude and your work habits improve tremendously over these past few months. On behalf of the Sonshine Christian School, please accept our gratitude."

Candice ogled the five hundred dollar check. "I don't think I can accept this."

Mrs. Pierce chuckled, "Of course you can. And I hadn't gotten to tell you, the board just approved a raise. You're doing an excellent job."

A stunned Candice left the office several minutes and a few Kleenexes later. She couldn't know her actions had saved her from a set of handcuffs later.

—◈—

Risk the possibilities of God. We cannot take courage alone, but we can do it with him. We don't need to worry about acceptance; Jesus accepts us when we show trust in him. He can make us irreplaceable right where we are.

A healthy fear of the Lord is the beginning of wisdom. Cooperation with the knowledge provided in the Bible can set us apart for a greater plan. We won't conduct ourselves perfectly, but when we mess up there are opportunities to make things right. Next, a little man with a strange name shows us how to start making ourselves irreplaceable.

——————— Investigative Questions ———————

1. Did you know times were appointed for you, including where you live, that you might seek God, though he is not far away from each of us? (Acts 17:26–27).

2. Do you know God declares the end from the beginning, from ancient times, things which have not been done, saying, "My purpose will be established?" (Isa. 46:10).

3. Do you have assurance of things hoped for, the conviction of things not seen? (Heb. 11:1).

Chapter 7

The Zacchaeus Zeal

Give more than you take.

"When you go somewhere, leave the place in as good or better condition than you found it," Dad said throughout my childhood. "It only takes a few minutes to make a big difference."

He taught me with hands-on experience. Side by side, my dad often helped me finish cleaning the kitchen once the dishes from our family of eight were washed. He would demonstrate the importance of attention to small details by showing me how to scrub behind and around the kitchen faucets. And he taught me never to put it off.

Sometimes, he'd ask me to help him with vehicle repairs or to lend a hand while he built things in the small shop behind our house. I learned the difference between a crescent wrench and a pipe wrench. He made plain the relevance of sweeping wood shavings off the floor and making sure the place was tidy before running off to play. "When you work for someone, treat their business as if you owned it," he often said.

But Dad wasn't the only parent who taught me the principles of good work ethics. "Don't put off what you can do now. You never know what might happen in the future, so take care of things while you can." Mom encouraged me to deny my instincts of procrastination.

My working-class parents passed their strong values to me, and I've successfully used their advice to rise to the top in many jobs. Much of their education came from experience, positive or negative consequences as a result of the choices they'd made. But as avid Bible readers, they also passed on millennia of Scriptural knowledge and taught me how to do the same.

Even when I doubted the validity of the Bible, I couldn't discount its proven outcomes from choosing good work ethics. Its examples of irreplaceable acts.

I've been working for as long as I can remember. Born the oldest of six children, some of my earliest memories take me back to changing diapers (cloth, not disposable). I would rinse the soil from them and then prepare for the daily ritual of washing them in our old wringer machine. My red, cracked hands shook in the frosty water during winter and broiled in the summer heat as I cranked the clothes through ancient rollers. It was disgusting and grueling work for a small child, but, as much as I hated it, I knew it had to be done.

In my early years, we were poor enough that my dad often killed wild game to put food on the table. My mom toiled in the garden to ensure we had vegetables and fruit. During the humid weeks of summer she harvested her crops. She mopped her face with a kitchen towel slung around her neck. Mom spent hours over boiling pots of mason jars, nestled inside her old pressure cooker. But we never went hungry. There were always plenty of frozen or canned goods to get us through harsh Missouri winters.

This is the classroom where I learned not to put things off. With eight people in the household, if we didn't do laundry, it piled into tall mounds, and, when we finally tackled it, the task was overwhelming. It felt like we'd never finish. Dishes were the same.

I wish I could say those good habits were so ingrained in me I've permanently overcome the problem of procrastination. But that would be a lie. I still fight a desire to do something that feels good before I've taken care of my responsibilities.

I guess that's why I identify with Frank's story so much. Let's see how he fares when faced with the temptation to put things off.

─∿─

Walking down the corridor, Frank paused by the large window facing east. Coral and lavender washed the horizon beyond Commerce Drive Clinic. Somewhere close, the buzz of an early morning lawn mower cranked to life. Frank couldn't wait to inhale the scent of fresh-cut grass. Even though it made him sneeze, he likened it to the soothing pleasure of warm rain on a spring day.

He glanced at his watch and quickened his steps, only forty-five minutes until shift end. He hurried to the nurse's station.

"Where have you been, Frankie?" Alex stopped moving her pen and looked up from the document she wrote on.

"Getting ready to call it a night." Frank stooped and leaned his forearms on the counter beside Alex.

"You didn't answer my question. You disappeared shortly after your shift started, and, now that it's almost over, you show back up. I don't see any reports in your hands." Alex cocked her left eyebrow.

"I'll get to them."

A sneer spread across Alex's face. "I heard John cleaned up after you last time. Don't expect me to."

"Did I ask you for anything?" Frank bristled at her bluntness.

"Not yet."

"I've still got time."

"While you're waiting for the right mood to strike, you can finish the assessment on our nausea patient in the waiting room."

Frank yawned, stood, and stretched his arms wide. "I've been at it all night. Someone else can write the assessment."

Alex opened her mouth, and got as far as, "You're not the only . . ."

The front doors crashed open. A woman screeched, "Help, somebody please help me."

Alex and Frank raced to the woman sagging against the door frame. She held the limp body of a small child. Frank did a mental eval as he took long strides toward the entryway. He estimated the child's age between three and four. Frank arrived first and reached for the pulse point on the petite, languishing arm. Relief stemmed his flow of adrenaline at the comforting feel of a thready thump on her little wrist.

The woman's elevated screams continued to throttle through the disinfected clinic air.

Frank gently touched her upper arm. "Ma'am, let me have the child."

"She's my baby." The woman clutched the toddler closer to her breast. "Can you save her?" Her terror-ridden eyes begged a yes answer.

Cautiously inching his hands toward the little girl's shoulders, Frank let his soothing words melt over her mother. "If you let me take her, we can evaluate her condition." He felt adult arms relax slightly from the child's lethargic form. "That's it, easy now, I've got her."

The mother released her grip, and Frank flashed into action. He whisked the child into an exam room, leaving Alex to call a doctor and comfort the grieving mother, even while she peppered the woman with diagnostic questions.

Seconds later, the doctor on call rushed into the room where Frank had just laid the child on a clean gurney. The physician yanked the chart from Frank's hand. He scanned the vitals information Frank had begun to note and pried the unconscious girl's left lid away from her eye. The doctor flicked a pen light up and down across the exposed retina. He murmured, "That's a good sign."

Frank moved closer.

"Vitals are sound."

The girl groaned. Her eyes popped open and she let out a frightened squeal. "Mommy. I want my mommy."

The mother swooshed the curtain back at the sound of her child's call. "I'm here, baby. Mommy's here." She cradled her daughter and rocked her back and forth, even as she shot a questioning look at the doctor.

"It's called syncope or, by its more common name, fainting. Relatively harmless and happens in a small percentage of children. Lying flat often remedies the problem."

"We'll do a few minor tests to be sure, but I think she'll be fine."

Less than two hours later, Frank helped the woman and her daughter with the discharge process. He moaned at the clock on the wall after he'd finally ushered them outside. Scratching his head and trying unsuccessfully to stifle yawns, he made his way to the employee locker room.

He had his scrub shirt half off his head when Rick, the clinic administrator, startled him. "Going somewhere?"

Frank tugged the scrub down far enough so he could see over the collar. "Long night."

"Doctor Russell told me about the fainter."

Frank unveiled his face, relaxed his grip on the scrub, and swooped it off his head in one smooth motion.

Rick furrowed his brows together. "I seem to be missing several of your reports." The administrator tapped a clipboard with his ink pen.

Frank hadn't seen the board before and something about the tap, tap, tap made him nervous. "There's a few I need to work on, but with nights like this, I can't seem to get caught up."

"Tonight was unusual. It's been relatively quiet around here the past few weeks. I don't have this problem with the other nurses, and I don't have time to hunt you down."

Feeling shaken, Frank scrambled for a response. "I'm sorry. I'll work on it."

"That's what you told me last time I had to address this with you."

"I promise, I'll get everything caught up before I go home."

"This is your last warning. If I have to talk to you again, just clean out your locker. We don't need dead weight around here."

Under Rick's watchful eye, Frank hurried to get dressed.

Knowing he was in trouble, he worked most of the day to finish the paperwork he'd put off. Exhausted, Frank finally shuffled home just after three. He was scheduled to start the next shift at eight. No time for sleep today.

Frank did better for a while. But over subsequent weeks, his consistency waned. Once the heat was off, Frank fell back into lethargic and sloppy habits.

Sixty days later, Rick visited Frank again. This time, there were no more chances.

Frank tried to keep his eyes from sweating tears. Rick stood over his shoulder, making sure everything was cleared from the locker. Commerce Drive Clinic no longer wanted Frank's service. He couldn't believe they were really letting him go.

—⁓—

Procrastination steals countless hours and untold dollars from companies around the globe. Every business that fails as a result of sloppy practices creates another domino in the ripple of a destructive economy. At the very least, individuals' choices to do less than they're capable of hurt their own chances of promotion. The worst scenario leads to job loss.

Timothy Pychyl described the phenomenon this way: "We make an intention to act, the time comes, but instead of acting we get lost in our own deliberation, making excuses to justify an unnecessary and potentially harmful delay. Who makes this decision? We do. The self, in fact, sabotages its own intention."[3]

In my estimation, such was the state of Zacchaeus when Jesus found him hiding high among tree branches. Zacchaeus didn't practice irreplaceable actions when Christ found him, but his willingness to change poor habits when discovered set him apart. He acted swiftly to correct what he'd done wrong, and he reacted with a surprising twist, willing to do far more than most of us can imagine.

When faced with his sin, Zacchaeus dared to be different. He chose the high road, and that made him irreplaceable. I imagine the scenario looked something like this.

Dust choked the air. People pushed and jostled to get a closer look at the street. Voices increased in pitch, and then the shouts, "There . . . isn't that him? I can see him, he's getting closer!"

Zacchaeus tried to stand on his tiptoes, but his stretched calves wouldn't lift him high enough. Then he hopped up and down. Sweat started beading on his face and down his back. He tried pushing through the crowd, but his efforts were no match for the jutting elbows and angry glares he encountered. In the throng, his expensive clothes and accessories meant nothing to the people. He was just another body fighting to get close—to him.

In defeat, Zacchaeus threaded his way to the back of the gathering. No one tried to stop his progress now. He looked at the backs of the mob, excitement building in their tone and jittery body language. Once again, he was an outsider looking in. He should be used to it by now. No one liked a tax collector, especially the chief, and no amount of money could buy him acceptance.

Zacchaeus always meant to make it up to them. He often told himself tomorrow he'd have enough money, and then he'd stop stealing from his fellow Israelites. He made mental promises to restore the hardship he put on others for his comfortable ways. But every morning when the sun rose, Zacchaeus simply put his good intentions off for another day.

In the excitement of the current moment, Zacchaeus didn't allow himself to dwell on regret. Pushing guilty thoughts from his mind was a well-practiced pattern. Without paying attention, he drove his conscience to its familiar dark corners. And concentrated on the man everyone was fighting to see.

He had one chance. He'd run ahead and see if he could find a place further down the road. When he reached a thinning in the crowd, he stopped. Panting, with streams of sweat pooling in the dirt below him, he saw it. Mighty and majestic, a perfect vantage point standing in the right location. He walked up to its trunk, tilted his head, craned his neck, and looked up at the imposing sycamore.

He thought to himself, it's a long way up. My robe might get caught, and I could lose my turban. If I'm seen, they'll make fun of me. What will they think? What if I get stuck? What if I fall?

Even worse—what if I miss my one chance to see him? I'm going for it!

He hiked his expensive gown and started up the tree. Zacchaeus grunted each time his arms pulled the weight of his body behind. Bark clawed his skin as he inched up the scratchy surface. His determination helped him push through the pain, the fatigue, and the fear, until finally, he reached the lowest limb. Zacchaeus swung his stubby legs over the branch and took a deep, cleansing breath. "Ahhh."

Minutes later, he could make out the figure heading in his direction. The crowds lining the road immediately closed behind the teacher as he passed their location. A swarm of bodies trailed for miles behind the ordinary-looking fellow. Though nothing about his features stood out, Zacchaeus noted the distinction in his smooth, confident gait. The essence of this man was different. Zacchaeus wasn't exactly sure what it was, but it was obvious.

His heart sped up, and his breath caught in his throat. The teacher who now stood almost directly under the limb, stopped cold, looked up, and locked eyes with him. "Zacchaeus, hurry and come down, for today I must stay at your house."

Zacchaeus couldn't believe it. The teacher not only wanted to talk to him, but he actually wanted to come to his house. And he didn't just want to come to his house; he wanted to stay at his house. Zacchaeus scurried down the tree, the descent much faster than the climb, with a grin plastered across his face.

Muttering and grumbling raced through the people who stood in the wake of the teacher. "He has gone to be the guest of a man who is a sinner." Many turned their backs and walked away. Others stood, mouths gaping in disbelief. Some shed tears of sorrow.

Zacchaeus remembered the guilty thoughts that plagued him earlier, and then he took action. "Behold, Lord, half of my possessions

I will give to the poor, and if I have defrauded anyone of anything, I will give back four times as much."

Jesus answered, "Today salvation has come to this house, because he, too, is a son of Abraham. For the Son of Man has come to seek and to save that which was lost."

The example provided by Zacchaeus is an interesting tale; you might have heard it in a child's church class or via a cute little song. But what does it have to do with procrastination? Does he teach us anything about becoming irreplaceable at work? I believe this story offers a secret key to unlock successful outcomes. In a single verse, Luke 19:8, Zacchaeus teaches us how to transform our attitudes:

- He made a public proclamation when he said, "Look, Lord . . ."
- He no longer put off what his conscience told him was right. Zacchaeus dedicated himself immediately to the change in his heart: "Here and now I give . . ."
- Zacchaeus humbly and unselfishly offered restitution and then some. Without being asked, he dedicated half his possessions to the poor. I imagine in addition to money, he would gladly have paid back four times the resources, the energy, and the time he stole from others.
- Zacchaeus's new work motivations resulted from a heart initiative. His attitude, not the work itself, saved him from loss (Luke 19:9).

I wonder what would happen if we used Zacchaeus's story as a prompt to give a hand to those poor in an area of work talents? What if we gave more effort, energy, and gratitude instead of hoarding selfishly? What might be saved? Our jobs?

Let's review Frank's story but add the elements of change demonstrated by Zacchaeus. Could it make a difference?

The buzzing of an early morning lawn mower caused Frank to stop by the east window at the Commerce Drive Clinic. He paused long enough to admire the horizon brushed with coral and lavender hues.

Fresh off the pages of his study about Zacchaeus, Frank determined not to let distraction prevent him from finishing his work today. He'd let things slip the past few months and, like Zacchaeus, planned to give back four times the amount of productivity he'd stolen. Because of procrastination, everyone at the clinic had suffered, and he wanted to make it up to them.

Frank decided to work through breaks and lunches and to put in extra hours each day until there was nothing left for him to give. He estimated he'd cost the clinic approximately sixty hours over the last year. He wasn't going to be legalistic about it, but he'd created a loss-time formula to help him calculate a reasonable amount to equal four times what he'd taken.

A few nights before, Frank sat down and plugged in his figures.

- Deduct thirty minutes every day in breaks
- Reduce from one hour to thirty minutes in lunch periods
- Add two extra hours before or after shift
- Calculate daily time repayment at three hours per day
- Multiply three hours times five work days for a weekly total of fifteen hours
- Tally the weekly total times sixteen weeks, coming up with 240 hours

He figured this would put him in the right range to repay his co-workers, his bosses, and himself for the time lost to procrastination.

Frank shuffled to the nurse's station where Alex studiously scratched on a page. He carefully walked behind her, trying not to break her concentration or his.

"Done with rounds?" Alex looked up.

"Sure am. I'll finish the report, and then I want to get back into my monthlies. I'm still behind."

Alex rested her mouth on the dry end of her ink pen and cocked her head. "What's got into you?"

"Nothing."

"Don't tell me nothing. How come you're all fired up to write reports and finish that paperwork you've let stack up over the past few months? Rick still on your back?"

Frank chuckled. "Nah, I just realized I owed the clinic some time."

"Just figured that out, huh?"

The retort stung Frank's ego, even as he recognized the truth of Alex's statement. "I didn't mean to cause extra burdens."

"If you want to lighten the load, you can do the assessment on our nausea patient in the waiting area."

Frank groaned but moved toward the hook holding the blank form. "Got it."

"Will wonders never cease?" the chair creaked as Alex leaned back and rocked.

"I'm making a change."

"Why?"

"I'm tired of doing to get. I've refocused my thinking. Now I get to do."

Alex pushed forward and leaned back over her report. "More power to you."

Frank quietly went to work. Until the screams of a frightened mother jolted him into action.

It was three hours before Frank saw the mother to the exit door with a sympathetic pat on her back.

"Thank you, mister." The pink-cheeked little girl appeared to have recovered from her fainting spell. Holding onto her mother's hand, she grinned at Frank past a yellow sucker.

He tousled her tawny hair, then watched the pair walk out the door. Now to get back to his paperwork. Frank was fast learning the value of taking care of things as soon as possible. He shook his head in thought. Better do what you can when you have the chance—you never know what life might hand you next.

Eight weeks into his new resolve, Frank got an unexpected visit from Rick, the clinic administrator.

Head in his clinic scrubs, Frank heard Rick before he saw him.

"Have you got a minute?"

Frank froze. He sounded muffled when he answered, "Uh, sure." He tugged the shirt back down.

Rick brought a clipboard from behind his back. "I wanted to talk about our numbers."

Frank turned cold from the inside out. "Numbers?"

"Why don't you finish dressing and come to my office?" Rick left Frank alone to ponder whether he'd have a job after the meeting.

Frank tapped on the glass office door.

"Come in."

Making his way to the chair across from Rick's desk, Frank exhaled while he hunkered into a sitting position.

"Do you know why I want to see you?"

Frank's voice trembled and he avoided eye contact. "No sir."

Rick ran his finger across a piece of paper in front of him, as if Frank could see the underlined information from his distance. "It says here that our numbers have changed in the past few months."

Frank shifted, and the chair squeaked beneath him.

Rick continued, "First, our Medicare and insurance payments were slow pay. It appears we weren't timely in filing our reports, and it delayed reimbursements. Do you know anything about that?"

Frank's toes began to fidget inside his shoes, and he rolled one foot in circles from the heel. "I let things get behind." Frank imagined the ax blow of being laid off.

Rick scooted his chair closer to the desk. "You think you impacted our bottom line by yourself?"

Puzzled by the question, Frank shrugged. "I can't change anyone but myself, but I am working on me. I hoped to prove I wasn't stuck in past patterns. I guess I waited too late."

Rick rose from his chair and walked to the window ledge behind his desk. He picked up a watering spout and trickled drops over the young, green shoot poking through black soil. With his back turned, Rick said, "I like your attitude. Tell me about these changes you've made."

Feeling a bit embarrassed, Frank talked to Rick's back and shared the Zacchaeus story. "Like Zacchaeus, I realized I need to pay back four times what I've stolen. Except instead of money, I took time and productivity through procrastination."

Rick put the spout down and turned.

Like a baby bird waiting for food, Frank's mouth was wide open and ready to speak his next sentence. But seeing Rick's eyes caused renewed terror to squeeze Frank's throat.

He prepared to hear the words he dreaded, "You're fired."

But Rick didn't speak. He wore a facial expression Frank couldn't quite read and then eased into his chair.

Frank suddenly became aware of the loud tick coming from the wall clock to his right. The only other sound in the room came from Rick flipping up pages from the clipboard on his desk. The same clipboard he'd hidden from view in the locker room. Maybe there was a pink slip buried in there.

Rick looked at Frank without raising his head, then glanced back at one of the pages. "Peculiar. When did you say you began this new practice?

"Never mind." Rick took his glasses off, and laid them on the desk. "Frank, do you know why I asked to talk to you today?"

"No."

"It wasn't public knowledge, but not too long ago, this clinic was in serious financial trouble. The board and I were struggling with how to keep the doors open. And then, about a month ago, money started coming in. Outstanding receivables poured into our account, and we were perplexed. I was tasked with sitting down with each individual employee to see if I could find out what happened. And now, you're telling me this crazy story. It doesn't make sense, but your timing matches the average period we'd expect payment to arrive after we send out invoices. Were you that far behind?"

Frank felt heat float up his neck. "Yes, sir."

Rick put on his glasses, got up, and pulled a filing drawer out. He lifted a folder and scanned the contents. Then he lifted another manila file and did the same. After looking at three different ones, he closed the drawer and turned. "It seems you aren't the only one who picked up the pace. A few other staffers started cleaning up their paperwork a couple of weeks after you. I guess this Zackie thing is working." Rick shook his head.

"Zacchaeus." Frank felt silly, but spoke anyway. "I actually call it the Zacchaeus Zeal."

"I don't care what you call it, don't stop." Rick scratched his temple. "I'm keeping my eye on you, Frank. I think you've got quite a future ahead of you. Thanks for making your changes and setting a good example. With people like you, we might just keep this place open after all." With that, Frank was dismissed.

Within six months, the clinic flourished financially, and Frank and his fellow employees received a bonus for their renewed efforts. Most of his co-workers didn't have a name for it, but many of them followed Frank's pattern and practiced the Zacchaeus Zeal.

Commerce Drive Clinic, its patients, and its employees received quadruple the benefits when Frank started a trend of giving back four times what he'd taken in the past. A trend that allowed everyone to benefit.

———

Frank learned to overcome the "buts" that held him back. How often do people say, "I'd do more around here, but. . . ." Or, "My work didn't used to pile up, but. . . ."

By offering ourselves a but excuse, we trap ourselves into a procrastination habit that grows with practice. At some point, we stop listening to what we're saying. The words are just another numbness-induced way to ignore a problem that eventually could cost us our jobs and maybe important relationships.

If, like Frank, you started noticing what you say and the habits you practice, might it make a difference? What if you took intentional steps to pay back what you owe?

To blast through procrastination, I have a little trick I play. I tell myself I'll only work five minutes on whatever activity I don't feel like doing. Whether it's exercise, cleaning my office, creating a spreadsheet, doing the dishes, or writing this book, I convince myself to invest a minimum of five full minutes of action on that project. The funny thing is, once I start, I often don't stop until I've made a great deal of progress or maybe even finished.

Consciously, I realize I'll often do more than I planned, but I can still jump-start myself psychologically. Much like Zacchaeus jumping from the tree with an action plan in mind, I can do the same with myself and stop procrastination in its tracks.

Beating procrastination and treating the property of others as if it were my own ensures a degree of favor in the workplace. But sometimes, our souls cry for more.

No matter how diligent we are, if we have placed ourselves in an improper job fit, a life of mediocrity is bound to haunt us. And the consequences reach far beyond the workplace.

In Chapter Eight, we'll tunnel to our deepest desires. What were you created for? Are you living in your purpose?

Turn the page to the Matthew Measure, and unearth all you are meant to do. Dig up your talents, invest them wisely, and watch your interest compound—discovering your natural abilities is the key to enjoying an abundant life.

—————— Investigative Questions ——————

1. Are your wages found in the life of the righteous? Or is your income that of the wicked—punishment? (Prov. 10:16).

2. Do you work hard in such a manner as to help the weak and remember the words of the Lord Jesus, "It is more blessed to give than to receive"? (Acts 20:35).

3. If you've stolen, have you committed to stealing no longer? Instead, do you labor, performing with your own hands what is good, so that you will have something to share with one who has a need? (Eph. 4:28).

Chapter 8

The Matthew Measure

Focus on what you can,
not on what you can't.

You have a special talent. Yes, you.

I promise you are endowed with at least one and maybe multiple things that set you apart from other people in meaningful ways. But how do you find it?

There seems to be a common thread to discovering your unique gift or gifts. Ask yourself this series of questions: What comes so naturally to me that I take it for granted and assume anyone can do it? What do people often request of me—at work, within my family, in my circle of friends or acquaintances? What do others brag about me that makes me feel ashamed because I know it's really no big deal, and I believe they are just being kind?

One of my great fascinations is human personality. I'm intrigued by the nuances, how they impact what we do, and how they make us feel about particular circumstances. I've studied the subject over multiple decades now, and it prompted me to become a certified personality trainer.

Years of research and study help me guide people to their best job fits. Though you cannot box someone into black-and-white categories, there are identifiable patterns of personality. Indicators of what we are naturally inclined to do well are rooted in our God-designed temperaments.

For example, though I admire those in the scientific profession, I have no desire or ability to glue myself to a petri dish for hours at a time. The level of patience and attention to minute detail required to accurately measure results are not natural for me.

With a great deal of effort and energy, I could push myself to learn, but, like forcing a square peg inside a round hole, the process would be rough, and the edges would never smooth. I'd probably give myself and others splinters while I tried to do the job. Any employer would gladly replace me with someone better suited. Why invest the effort and energy in unnatural conditions?

Yet I have friends who analyze laboratory data who don't understand my desire to sit in front of a computer making up scenarios. They could care less about correct spelling or grammar. For them, any word might do.

We all have strengths and weaknesses, and we all have special talents. But some of us allow life to shovel piles of dirt over our gifts until we no longer see them. We live with a sense of inadequacy that prevents us from pursuing God-given abilities and dreams.

Many of us subsist in mediocre jobs that feel like drudgery to perform. There is no spark, excitement, or anything to look forward to. We blame our employers, our fellow employees, and the work, when often the problem lies within. In a deep spot, where our gifts and meaning for existence lie dormant.

We fail to achieve what we were created for. We miss the opportunity to become irreplaceable.

I believe we were all born to fulfill a great purpose. Doctors save lives. Quality inspectors protect us from dangerous equipment problems. Teachers enable us to read so we can gain knowledge. Artists inspire us. Friends and family lift us up when we're down. Parents can love, even when we behave in unlovely ways.

If we fail to uncover our high calling, that thing that sets us apart from most people we know, our parting words may ripple with regret before we leave this earth. There is no sadder outcome than to die without living up to your potential.

Dennis, though successful on the outside, was unhappy in his chosen profession. His talents were buried deep and hidden under many layers of poorly invested energies. His sad story resonates with far too many.

—~~—

The first time Dennis knew the feeling of inadequacy, he was five years old. The middle child of three, his heart sank when his mother glowed over his three-year-old sister's drawing of their happy family. The scruffy little towhead ran to his secret hideout and cried for a very long time.

Dennis knew his older brother and younger sister shared their mother's aptitude. They oohed over her paint-scented art room filled with easels, charcoals, and colorful acrylics. A sketched lion, with a thickly penciled mane hung next to a rainbow of fruit brush-stroked into a painted ceramic bowl. Ballerinas danced, mountain streams flowed, and strangers smiled. All created by Dennis's mother.

Even his father showed an artistic flair when sculpting wood. It seemed everyone in the house could craft something beautiful. Everyone except Dennis.

It wasn't for lack of effort. He carried reams of paper to his hideout. He snuck charcoal pencils and a few paints from his mother's art room. As early as kindergarten, he amassed a stock of #2 pencils. All of these items he secreted to his clubhouse—where the little boy practiced drawing stick people for minutes, hours, and days at a time.

He dug into his upper lip with a youthful underbite. Furrowed eyebrows helped him concentrate. Dennis broke numerous lead tips as he practiced attaching stick legs to stick torsos. Sweat dripped onto smudged portraits that looked more like malformed globs than faces.

By the time Dennis turned fifteen, he'd flunked or dropped out of three different art classes. He felt like a complete loser. It seemed everything he tried was tainted by what he couldn't do.

Dennis was sure he didn't have any special gifts. He wondered why he was born. He thought there must be a secret something wrong with him, that God didn't like him and had passed him over because he didn't deserve good things. Dennis developed habits based on this misguided bias and carried them into adulthood.

After college, Dennis's older brother landed a job as a graphic artist for a famous apparel company. Their younger sister mixed her passion for helping people with a natural artistic talent and entered the field of art therapy.

Dennis, bored and disappointed, quit college after one semester. He hopped from job to job but couldn't find anything that interested him enough to stick it out for long.

His separations were typically mutual. Without the drive to get out of bed for something he enjoyed, a few weeks into the job, Dennis often overslept. Knowing his no-show, no-call pattern meant dismissal, he'd simply apply for another position that paid enough to cover the rent and make his car payment.

In his late twenties, Dennis's brother used his connections to get him on at the apparel company. The money was better than previous jobs, and soon he pulled down a decent salary. It was just enough to get him out of bed in the mornings.

But Dennis never felt like he fit into the easy flow of the creative minds around him. He learned how to negotiate prices and schedules as a textile buyer, but his proficiency didn't bring happiness. An unknown emptiness plagued him from somewhere deep inside his gut. The money and accolades were okay, but often he still dreaded going to work.

It seemed in a blink, twenty-seven years passed. Dennis knew textiles seam to seam. Now in his early fifties, he made great money, had a solid reputation, but still struggled. Deep down, he couldn't get rid of a dark discontent.

Years of emotional stress over perceived failures had taken their toll. He wouldn't have the job if it weren't for his brother. He wasn't gifted like his family. Dennis felt like an outsider wherever he went.

His emotional symptoms took on physical traits. Dennis walked hunched over, as if carrying the weight of the world on his back. His joints and muscles barked when he sat down or got up. His older brother looked fifteen years his junior. Intestinal issues made eating food of any kind a miserable endeavor.

And Dennis's personal relationships fared no better. Three divorces, four estranged children, and three rarely seen grandchildren left him bitter and lonely. Dennis struggled through each day with the same lethargic survival skills. He felt like a dead man walking, but apathy prevented him from doing anything different. Dennis had given up on himself years before—now he existed and watched other people live while he pretended.

———

Success on the surface does not mean we are doing what we are created for. Many of us labor to become irreplaceable where we are but—no matter how hard we try and even when we accomplish our goals—feel a weight of dissatisfaction. This may indicate an improper job fit.

But be careful of a quick diagnosis. You cannot identify a poor fit from a single occurrence or two. You also cannot trust a purely emotional response. However, a consistent state of discontent coupled with having to expend extreme amounts of energy and effort to complete tasks may reveal symptoms of enduring a job you aren't naturally suited for.

And if the job doesn't fit, misery is sure to follow.

No amount of money is worth the toll it takes when you feel dissatisfied inside. Until we identify and invest in our high calling, we cannot become irreplaceable.

On my website, www.brooksanita.com, I offer several tools to help you identify your natural job fit. Whether fun, adventurous, artistic, or simple define your ideal work environment, I believe unearthing your talents is worth the effort.

But, once you know what work you are best suited for, how do you know what to do with your talent? Through parables, short stories with lessons embedded in them, the Bible shows us how to overcome our weaknesses and develop our strengths. One such parable, in Matthew 25, steers us toward our high calling. The Master's instruction equips us to become irreplaceable. Here's what we can learn:

- Leaders often turn their possessions over to subordinates for safekeeping (Matt. 25:14).
- Talents are given based on individual ability so they can be invested and multiplied (Matt. 25:15–17).
- Some go off by themselves, dig a hole, and hide their talents (Matt. 25:18).
- There are rewards for investing our talents for the benefit of those we serve (Matt. 25:19–23).
- Assumptions and fear can cause us to hide our talents and keep us from receiving potential rewards (Matt. 25:24–26).
- When we deposit our talents with the right sources, the original investment compounds with interest (Matt. 25:27).
- Refusal to unearth our talents and put them to good use can cause us to lose what we have (Matt. 25:28–30).

One of the key elements of this particular passage lies in verse 27, where we are reminded to deposit our talents with the bankers. Asking God for direction on whom to invest with can mean success, whereas denial of his power can result in a loss of livelihood. But taking the courage to start over isn't easy.

Job interviews are hard on the soul. Trying to anticipate the next question and preconceive your next pithy answer—it's easy to miss the full scope of the request just asked.

Heart palpitations, shortness of breath, films of sweat, attempts to sneak looks to take in the nuances of the place, and nervous tics often distract us from paying close attention to the interviewer.

Anxiety is a natural result when we need a job. There's a reason the Bible says to take courage. We must clutch it when we're nervous.

But nerves or not, we give our best interviews when they reflect core values of honesty, humility, and a teachable heart. Otherwise, even if you get the position, once you are comfortable, your true nature will shine through anyway. A flavor of deception doesn't bode well for long-term employment and often keeps you from being hired to begin with. What we think we hide luminates past the edges of our masks.

Besides, the interview is the best time to find out if this is the right job fit. Neither you nor the potential employer will be happy trying to force a square peg into a round hole. It can be done, but, in the long run, the edges will be ragged and will cause splinters to shred the emotions of everyone affected.

Jobs that allow us to utilize God-given aptitude ensure we thrive, whatever we do. Dennis was transformed from a life of lethargy to purpose-induced joy when he acted on his unique abilities. But first, he had to take courage and change out of his comfort career. The first move proved the hardest one of all.

———

The only life Dennis knew was in the shadow of his family's artistic talent. At thirty-four years old, he was the only one who didn't jabber at holidays, parties, and other celebrations about his exciting career or hobby. Dennis didn't understand the big deal about all their artsy talk anyway.

It took an uncontrollable circumstance for Dennis to do anything different.

On vacation in Florida, he stepped into the condo's pink-tiled shower. He picked up a bar of Irish Spring and took a full sniff. As he was lathering up, a loud jolt of thunder caused him to drop the bar onto the white rubber mat under his bare feet. Dennis was sure he felt the building shake.

He reached for the slimy green and white rectangle beside his foot and put it back in place. Dennis reached for the shampoo to slather onto his scalp. He scrubbed with his fingers, then reached up and adjusted the metal shower head to propel enough water to rinse his hair. Instantly, the bathroom turned black.

Dennis had no idea how long he had lain crumpled in the corner of the shower stall when he forced his stinging eyes open. He was sure the smell of smoke mixed with Irish Spring was in his head. He tried to sit, but, between the slippery tub floor and a searing shoulder, he couldn't push himself up.

It felt like infinity before he could garner the strength to roll onto his left side and leverage himself to a stand. He stumbled through nausea and shaky muscles to call 911.

At the hospital, the emergency room physician analyzed the deep burn piercing Dennis's right palm and the matching one that exited the shoulder on the same side. "You are a lucky young man. I've seen my share of lightning strikes, but not all victims survive."

Dennis groaned while a nurse prodded his shoulder wound. "What time is it?"

The doctor rolled his wrist. "Six forty."

Not thinking, Dennis tried to sit up. "It wasn't even four o'clock when I got in the shower. How long was I out?"

"The blast couldn't have lasted more than milliseconds. Most of the strike passes over the surface of the body in a process called external flashover. Most likely, you were knocked out either from the lightning's force or when you were thrown back."

"My chest feels like somebody hit me with a cannonball."

"We'll run a few tests on your heart."

"Should I be worried?"

"I'll know more when I get your results. But I can tell you this much, if you believe in God, he was watching out for you today."

Dennis closed his eyes. He'd intentionally avoided thoughts of God for most of his adult life.

After his release the next afternoon, Dennis stopped at a bookstore and then spent the rest of his vacation holed up in the condo. He'd never read anything from a Bible before, and the more he studied, the deeper his conviction. He gave in to it on Thursday.

Dennis sat in a deck chair, salty breezes blowing through his hair. He looked past a pure blue sky, where white thunderheads gathered on the horizon, giving him goose pimples. "I'm not sure if I'm doing this right, but, Jesus, I need you to forgive me. You said, if I believed and trusted you as the one who could save me from my mistakes, I could have eternal life. I do believe, and I want you to make me a better person. Please help me."

He wasn't sure why he smiled, but it came from the inside out.

When Dennis arrived home, he searched for a church. He continued reading the Bible every day, but soon an old problem cropped up with a new twist.

The more he studied, Dennis couldn't avoid the message threaded throughout passage and verse. It seemed God was telling Dennis he should have a special gift or talent. But what could it be?

Dennis was the inartistic child born into a family of artists. The deep sense of inadequacy he'd fought his entire life continued into his Christian experience. He wasn't good at anything.

And to make things harder, every time he read a book, listened to the radio, or talked to someone else, the Parable of the Talents in Matthew 25 came up. Each incidence caused a twist of guilt in his gut. He asked God to either release him from the guilt or reveal a talent he might have.

He wrote on an index card, "What is my talent?" and posted it on his bathroom mirror. Each time he saw the card, he prayed and asked God to reveal the mystery.

It took almost a year for the answer to arrive.

Sitting in a pew, half listening to the sermon as he scanned his Bible, a quiet voice seemed to whisper into his mind. "Your talent has been under your nose all along."

Stunned, Dennis flinched, then looked around.

No one seemed to notice.

The voice continued, "You've spent your life focused on what you don't do well, instead of paying attention to the gifts you have."

"What gifts? You didn't give me any," Dennis argued in his mind.

"It comes so naturally, you don't even realize it's a talent."

"Please tell me, what am I missing?"

"What do friends and family ask you for help with more than anything else?"

Dennis concentrated. "I truly don't know what you're talking about."

"Letters, English assignments, and other writing projects? Doesn't your boss ask you to write his memos and doctor his e-mails?"

"Anyone can do those things."

"Are you sure? Ask people. If it's so easy, why don't they simply write their own?"

And there it was. Dennis's special gift. So easy for him that Dennis didn't see it as extraordinary.

But the revelation didn't tell him what to do with it.

After church, Dennis pored over every word in Matthew 25. When he came to verse 27, an idea sparked.

But wasn't it too late? At his age, with no formal education, how could Dennis successfully deposit his talent with the appropriate bankers? Who were they? How did an aspiring writer get started?

Once again, he wrote his question on an index card and posted it on his bathroom mirror. Dennis didn't tell anyone about his quest.

Each morning and evening he prayed over the words, "Who are the bankers you want me to invest my talent with?"

Like before, the answer did not come swiftly.

A few months later, in a passing conversation, a friend said, "I've got a buddy in New Mexico going to a writer's conference. Craziest thing, I never knew he was a writer."

Dennis's breathing sped up. Adrenaline pulsed through his body. "Where'd you say this conference is?"

His friend made direct eye contact. "Why?"

Dennis shuffled his feet and tried to pull back the tears welling in his eyes. The power of his emotional reaction made him stammer. "I think, . . . nah, it's silly."

"You're a writer?"

"Not yet. I'd just like to check it out."

"I'll get you his contact info."

"I'd appreciate it."

Dennis drove home feeling terror and excitement all mixed together.

Less than forty-eight hours later, he'd signed up, before he talked himself out of it.

When he arrived in New Mexico, Dennis turned the radio on in the rental car. Maybe music would loosen his taut nerves on the drive from the airport to the conference facility.

But on arrival, he immediately felt an old tug on his heart. The foyer was crowded with smiling, hugging people, all wearing excited looks on their faces. The scene reminded him of family get-togethers. He was the outsider looking in.

With a fresh breath of resolve, Dennis stepped forward. He spotted a sign hanging over a busy desk that said, "Register here," and walked toward it.

Waiting in line, a man's voice spoke behind him. "First time?"

"That obvious?"

The man offered a handshake. "I'm Lou. Feel free to sit next to me at dinner tonight. I'll show you the ropes."

Dennis pumped Lou's hand and expelled pent up air. "I really appreciate it."

"Next," a harried looking woman yelled from behind the desk. But she offered a gentle smile when she handed over his conference materials.

Looking through the registration packet, Dennis walked outside and tried to make sense of the hand-drawn map in his hand. A clasp on his shoulder made him jump.

"Where have they got you?" Lou grinned.

"I'm trying to figure that out."

"Mind if I take a look?"

"Please." Dennis gratefully shoved the folder of paperwork toward Lou.

"You're in Control."

Dennis pursed his lips. "I'm definitely not in control."

Lou's belly laugh echoed across the campus. "Sorry. It's the name of your room. You're assigned to the outbuilding called Control. Follow me, I'm a couple of rooms over."

Feeling rather dumb, Dennis quietly fell in step as Lou walked them to a set of rustic-looking cabins, cowboy-style bunkhouses, actually. Lou promised to be back at four thirty to walk with Dennis to the cafeteria. In the meantime, Dennis settled in Control.

Over the next three days, Dennis experienced a hurricane of activity. His mind felt battered with whirling bits of information. Differing opinions about the business of writing, tip sheets, formulas, book recommendations. He carried armfuls of information to his room each evening.

But what really blew him away was the surprising amount of encouragement he received. Dennis hadn't realized when he signed up that a benefit of attending a conference was face-to-face appointments with agents, editors, and publishers. With nothing to offer, Dennis honestly explained he only came to learn. He asked questions, and the professionals across the table from him responded with enthusiastic guidance.

Dennis left the conference knowing his life would never be the same. On the flight home, he replayed some of the professional comments that stuck in his mind.

"I see real promise from the sample you submitted in my class."

"You definitely have a gift. Just remember that diamonds require cleaning and polishing before they sparkle. Writing is no different. Scrub away the impurities through education and practice, then your gift will shine."

"Don't give up. It's one of the biggest mistakes most writers make."

"My best advice is to learn everything you can about the craft of writing. That's your foundation."

"A lot of people think and talk, but not many do. Be a doer, and you will leap ahead most of the crowd."

"Seek God's kingdom first—he will direct your path."

A few days after Dennis settled back into the everyday world, he got on his knees and asked God to mentor him. He vowed to put Bible study and prayer first, before attempting anything else. Then he began the practical steps to turn his dream into a reality—with God's help.

Dennis continued in his role as a textile buyer to pay the bills and support his newly realized talent. He cut back on extras and spent the money on writing investments. He bought books on the craft of writing and devoured them. He signed up for classes and poured himself into applying everything he learned.

Several months later, Dennis entered his first writing contest and though he didn't place, he scoured the winning entries. Afterward, he thought himself better equipped for the next one.

During the same period, he went through his stacks of paper from the conference and found the submission guidelines for a prominent ministry. Dennis wasn't sure what he would write a devotional about, so he asked God for advice.

The next day, Dennis woke up feeling inspired. He sat down and poured his heart into a short story based on his past feelings of inferiority. After a brief prayer, he e-mailed the document to the editor listed on the guidelines page.

Six days later, his in-box relayed exciting words.

Dear Dennis,

When I read your devotional, "Painting Pictures with Words," I knew it was something we could use. Many people will receive a blessing from your honest account of struggle and hope. I plan to publish it within the next sixty days and will provide details in advance. Thank you for the submission.

Sincerely,
Jane Tarp
Associate Editor, CBN.com

Dennis next took the leap and submitted six different query letters to various publications. Amongst the rejections and nonresponses, he was surprised to get a positive reaction. One periodical asked to see the manuscript. It took nine months for him to see his article in print, but finally the day arrived.

Dennis now had two bylines to his credit. These small victories gave Dennis the courage to take another step toward the dream he most wanted to turn into reality.

Hidden in a deep part of his heart, Dennis wanted to write books.

So he invested time and energy into diversifying his talent.

During the day, he started with Bible study before heading off to work as a textile buyer. When he came home at night, after dinner, he worked hard at his driving passion. The thing that made him smile and laugh more. The thing that instilled excitement and made him want to be a better man. The thing that propelled him to be a more productive employee at the apparel company.

The thing that also made him feel like giving up at least ten times a day.

Dennis studied the details of writing books and practiced the craft of good proposals. He began to build a writing business and learned how to manage it wisely. At every step, Dennis asked God who the bankers were, who should he invest his talents with?

Dennis reworked one particular book proposal at least a dozen times over an eighteen-month period. And then opportunity beckoned. A reputable literary agency agreed to look at his work and, within the month, signed Dennis.

After eight months, his book sold to a royalty publishing house.

Two years later, when his fingers caressed the cover of his first published book, Dennis cried tears of joy. The Master had compounded the interest on Dennis's efforts.

Free from the trap of comparing himself to others, Dennis relaxed in most areas of his life. He applied for a lateral move to a copywriting position at the apparel company. And though he squirmed, he made it through a multilevel interview process.

His first book didn't make him rich, but, as he published more and accepted public speaking requests, his income grew. Eventually enough that he quit his day job altogether and wrote copy as an independent contractor while he continued to write and sell books.

At one of his speaking engagements, he met a mocha-haired beauty named Anna. Less than a year later, he looked deep in her onyx eyes and said, "I do."

Time passed for Dennis, filled with much peace and contentment. He and Anna raised three children and ultimately welcomed grandchildren. Looking back, he could see how unearthing his talent had changed his life.

By grace, he'd dug it up, invested, and earned interest, so the Master could multiply the rewards. Dennis was created to paint pictures with words. And to think, he almost missed his chance—by focusing on what he couldn't do.

There is great hope in living a meaningful life, but the definition looks different to each of us, based on natural ability, personality, life experience, and God-endowed opportunity. It's up to us to seek a meaningful living as individuals. To find the role that makes us irreplaceable.

Hope and meaning give us a reason to get out of bed each morning.

Even when our day jobs don't feel important, they may offer the resources we need to help us learn what we are meant to do.

If you bury your unique talent, not only do you suffer, but those around you suffer from the loss of what you might offer. The world brightens when one person's distinctive talent is unearthed and brought into the light of daily use. A diamond only sparkles after it is unearthed, cleaned, and polished.

What have you buried? Isn't it time to start digging, so you can invest with the bankers? Ask your Master for help; he's waiting to share his happiness. It's the miracle of living in your purpose.

Good leaders know you can't experience a miracle if you don't first have a problem. As we look ahead, we'll unravel a mystery in the midst of mayhem.

———— Investigative Questions ————

1. Do you know that your gifts and call from God are irrevocable? (Rom. 11:29).

2. Are you using your different gifts according to the grace given to us by faith? (Rom. 12:6).

3. Does your life testify by signs, wonders, and various miracles and by gifts of the Holy Spirit distributed according to God's will? (Heb. 2:4).

PART THREE

Leadership Principles

Chapter 9

The Moses Management

Without a problem,
there are no miracles.

Are you responsible for anything?

If so, you are managing. And managing guarantees problems.

We are all managers, though not everyone carries the formal title. Many of us are called to steward projects, time, jobs, people, materials, or money. Regardless of what we manage, the goal is to move something forward, toward a particular destination. But forward movement does not ensure success and won't necessarily make you irreplaceable.

In our desire to move ahead, we sometimes avoid things or people perceived to slow us down. Problems. And consequences occur when we put off dealing with a difficulty or impulsively react to it.

This is where we get in trouble. And how we miss our miracles.

Impulsiveness and problem avoidance are common mistakes for managers, me included. We desire a certain end but, in our hurry to get around the wall in front of us, fall back on an easier way out.

But easier isn't necessarily faster. Often, the more difficult, direct route through a problem is the best and quickest answer.

Below are the three most common easy answers I, and other managers, make:

1. Slap a Band-Aid over a wound without first cleaning out the dirt
2. In efforts to head down the highway, ditch-hop from one rut to another
3. Shower once, expecting permanently clean results

What do these three vastly different analogies have in common? Let me explain.

Band-Aids: We hurry to fix our problems. But in our scramble to repair the damages, we sometimes throw a bandage over the wounded area without cleaning out the dirt. Unless we scrub out the impurities, down to the root of the damage, we unwittingly ask for staph infections.

The original wound can spread disease to others. Under the Band-Aid, impurities swell and create oozing discontent. Just because we cover something doesn't mean it's hidden.

Ditch-hopping: My second example isn't always obvious. I've often made this mistake with personal decisions as well as in the workplace.

We recognize we have a problem, made a mistake, or need to improve. We analyze current conditions, and set our sights on a new destination. We're going to hit the highway and move toward a new and better destination.

But more often than not, we overcorrect. We overthink the necessary changes and jump over the highway only to land in the opposite ditch. We do things differently all right, but we're still stuck in a rut.

Communication showers: If you shower once, does it mean you're clean the rest of your life?

Of course it doesn't.

Too often, we believe of ourselves and others that a single instruction should knock the dust off and cleanse us of past mistakes. So why do we assume a single conversation to address a problem, a one-time meeting, or an annual evaluation is enough to keep mind-sets clear and on course? The human brain is wired in such a way that it needs consistent refreshers.

In past decades, we've seen a shrinking workforce expected to handle increasing job responsibilities. Cutbacks, reengineering, layoffs, downsizing, restructuring, or whatever else you call it results in stressed employees pushed to insane measures. The state of our current economic culture increases the risk of using easy outs like Band-Aids, ditch-hopping, and fewer communication showers.

The pressure to move fast and do more with less spreads any organization or business thin. In that culture, we miss important elements, making it harder to distinguish between doing a job poorly or doing it well. It also negatively impacts the morale of those required to get the job done and adds tension to those who manage their efforts.

The frightened recipients are desperate for a savior. They want a miracle maker.

But who's there to be the savior? What happens when managers try every tactic and yet nothing works? They keep circling around until they end up at the same place—desperate for their own miracle.

As the head pastor of Harvest Home, a growing church, Josh's problems were mounting. As the pressures built, so did Josh's burnout. Let's observe his management process and see whether there's a miracle in the making.

―◊―

The hall echoed with a dark 5 A.M. quiet. Josh flicked his thumb against the wall plate. A domino of florescent squares pinged down the corridor, washing the walls in white.

Joshua Conners reread the three text messages that were keeping him up at night while he stumbled toward the office. He desperately needed a caffeine fix this morning.

He groaned at the stack of folders waiting on his desk. But they'd have to wait longer. Bigger problems demanded attention. He wished he could run away. Josh felt like he'd hit a brick wall.

Harvest Home was growing faster than Josh could keep up with. It required long hours to administrate employees, nurseries, teen tracks, singles, young marrieds, homeless ministries, parenting classes, marriage counseling, senior meals, weddings, funerals, the new Family Life Center, and Christian book club, along with multi-demographic Sunday school classes and Bible studies. None of this included the practical need to stay on top of the church's finances, scheduling, building maintenance, and more. There were boards, staff, and committees, but Josh oversaw the bigger vision for them all. He was supposed to have it all together.

His answer? Like a CEO of any large corporation, he worked harder, longer, and more intently.

Josh powered his MacBook then brushed his fingers across the smiling faces of his family. A lonely grin shadowed his lips.

Josh had barely glanced at the audit report when his cell rang.

Strain laced the elder female voice on the other end. "Pastor Conners, this is Sarah Davis. I'm at the hospital with Matt. He had a heart attack last night. Can you come right away?"

Josh hesitated, looking from the stacks piled on his desk to the report on his computer screen and, finally, the full calendar in front of him.

"Are you there?" Sarah said.

"I'm sorry, yes. I'll leave now."

He printed the e-mail and audit report, then threw them into his briefcase with a few of the folders on his desk. Josh pushed the remaining papers to the side, jotted a list for his secretary to follow up on, and headed out the door. He was gone most of the morning.

On his return, Josh was disappointed to walk in on Darlene, hunkered and hushed in phone conversation—again. He didn't mean to snap so loud, but he was tired of it. "Is that a work-related call?"

In milliseconds, her neck sprouted thick, red lily pads. Welts the size of bamboo shoots shot across her pale skin. "I've gotta go," she hissed into the receiver. But at least she did turn away from the phone and toward her computer screen.

Josh crossed the threshold into his office and slammed the door. Guilt flooded his veins as he slumped into the chair behind his desk.

His phone pinged with a new text message. Five total in the past three days. Two in the last hour. The sender demanded his attention. He could avoid it no more and dialed.

The second ring was interrupted by Ted Foster's voice. "Are you going to address it?"

"We've got to consider the younger generations. They prefer more contemporary music."

"They're irreverent, that's why. I liked it better when we were smaller. More personal that way."

"I need to approach this carefully. I don't want to offend."

"But you don't care about offending those of us who made our church what it is today. You want to kick us to the curb."

Josh propped an elbow on the desktop and let the side of his head fall onto his open palm. "That's not true. People like you are the backbone of our congregation."

"Don't patronize me."

Josh sighed, "My intent is not to patronize you. I'm trying to figure out how to mix two different worlds."

"Hmph."

The line died in Josh's hand. He was grateful.

Feeling a fresh bath of guilt for his earlier outburst, Josh got up and opened the door. He peeked around the corner and smiled at Darlene. "How would you like a lemon poppy-seed?" It was Darlene's favorite. "I need some fresh air."

She scratched her head with the ink pen in her hand. Her voice echoed with a tint of sarcasm, though she kept her tone respectful. "I don't want to cause any trouble."

Josh ignored it and hoped his gesture offered an appropriate apology. "Be back in a jiffy."

Darlene's forehead crinkled as she furrowed her brow and watched Josh walk toward the door.

He was pretty sure he heard her mumble, "Never says, 'I'm sorry,'" toward his back as he exited.

Josh turned and started to say something to make his own point. But changed his mind. It wouldn't do to have her stay mad at him.

Lately, he seemed to walk in circles, where he'd snap at his secretary and then try to make up for it. He knew he came across as weak one minute and a snarling tyrant the next. At night he tossed and turned, playing out scenarios of what he wished he'd said earlier in the day.

Josh prayed while he walked to and from the bakery. He desperately wanted to handle things better. Why couldn't he get a grip?

Back at the office, he handed Darlene her muffin and took his cinnamon crunch bagel with him. Josh didn't miss the *People* magazine scrunched beneath the church bulletin layout. "Getting a lot done?" Heartburn fired in Josh's belly.

There was an edge to her answer. "Of course."

Josh ignored the impulse to call her out and escaped quickly to the refuge of his office. He sat down behind the desk and opened his briefcase. On top of the bulging hill of papers, he pulled the printed copies of the audit report and committee notes. Yellow highlights were painted all over the ledger, revealing an unwanted surprise.

Tomorrow's financial meeting wouldn't be fun.

Josh's cell phone rang again. He was relieved to see Ian Hagis's name. Maybe Ian could shed some light on Josh's struggles. The elder man was available and drove right over.

Josh settled in beside Ian in one of the two brown chairs across from the oak laminate desk. "The pressure's getting to me. Sometimes I feel like an invisible knee is shoved against my chest. When it happens, I can't catch my breath. Makes me wonder if I'm going to have a heart attack or stroke."

Ian turned in his chair so his entire body faced Josh, "I know exactly what you mean. It's a panic attack. Used to get 'em all the time." Ian nodded knowingly. "Ever feel like you've been thrown into a black hole? You try to climb out, but the sides are slimy, and all you do is slip back down?"

Josh straightened in his chair. "Exactly. You get it." He almost reached out and embraced the man.

Ian's face turned reflective. "Yeah, let me tell you . . ."

Josh's countenance slumped. For the next hour and a half, he listened to Ian's tales of woe.

When the older man finally announced his departure, he first stood at the door and patted Josh's shoulder. "Thanks for listening. I feel a heap better getting some of this off my chest."

Josh simply nodded and smiled faintly. The weight on his own chest felt heavier than ever.

Determined not to let anxiety get the best of him, Josh went back to his desk. High on his to do list was preparing the Sabbath sermon.

After wasting too much time in a struggle to write something fresh, Josh relented. He hated to do it again but pulled an old sermon from a dated computer file. By moving a few things around, replacing the real-life story with a more current version, and adding an extra verse, his members wouldn't know the difference.

Josh knew he was a fraud.

A light tap, tap, tap interrupted his self-deprecation.

A lovely smile on the face in the doorway lifted Josh's own lips. He was surprised his wife had left the house.

"Got time for a lunch date?"

Josh's stomach clenched. He didn't really have time, but he overrode the instinctual knot. "For you? Always."

His wife sighed, "I wish."

They went to the cafe around the corner for a modest meal of soup and sandwiches.

After ordering, Bianca revealed the reason for her spontaneous visit. "Charlene, from across the street, is watching Mom."

"I wondered how you got away."

"The doctor called."

Josh didn't like the melancholy reverberating in her words.

Bianca gripped his fingers over the table. "It's breast cancer."

A subzero blast blew through Josh's entire body. Any response froze on his lips.

Tears slipped off Bianca's cheeks.

The waiter brought their food but could have served it to any other patrons. Neither took a bite.

Josh called the office and told Darlene he needed to take care of an important personal matter. Then he went home to mourn with his wife.

After Bianca put her mother to bed, they curled up on the couch. Wrapped in shock and each other's arms, they cried more than they talked.

The next morning, Josh gently unraveled himself from his wife's arms. He looked at the crooked smile on her sleeping mouth. He wished he could crawl back in bed and stay with her forever.

Josh sleepwalked through his workday. Darlene finally stopped asking whether he wanted to take calls and automatically told people he wasn't available. He called Bianca every hour until two thirty.

The last time, she chuckled courageously into the receiver. "If I wasn't depressed before, I will be if you don't stop calling. We haven't talked on the phone this much in a year."

Josh hated the reminder.

That evening, after forcing down a few bites of dinner, Josh kissed his wife and forced himself to leave for the church meeting.

Perfunctory prayers, introductions, and reports took twenty minutes, then the audit committee took over.

The paper in the chairwoman's hands shook. "Tithes and offerings are down nearly 30 percent from this time last year."

A murmur echoed from the back.

"We squeezed the budget last year."

"Can we cut some of our class materials?" Alice Ray spoke from a middle pew.

John Aubrey raised his hand. "We already started making our members pay for most of their own books."

"Aren't our attendance numbers up? Shouldn't that mean more money coming in?" a timid voice dared.

Ted Foster stood.

Josh stifled his groan.

"Some of us aren't writing the checks we used to. I'm going to put it plain. It's time newer folks stepped up and helped foot the bill, instead of puttin' their hands out. Why aren't any of them here tonight?"

Josh stood and used his hands to demonstrate peace. Like rain falling down in "The Itsy Bitsy Spider." "Let's not say something we'll regret."

"Of course you're gonna side with 'em. You like that irreverent noise they call music too. Well, you can have it. And you can pay for it."

"That's pretty harsh, don't you think?"

The deacon faced him man to man. "Our church has been in a rut for a while. We need a leader who's not afraid to lead."

Church members stood up throughout the sanctuary. Some in defense of Josh, some siding with Foster. A face-off ensued. The sanctuary turned into a chamber of accusations and rage. Several folks slipped meekly out the side door. Factions fought factions, and Josh stood helpless in the middle.

By the time the small crowd dispersed, Josh knew a split was imminent.

A few weeks later, Matt, who'd had the heart attack right before the eruption in their church, relapsed and died. His wife, Sarah, asked Josh to preach the funeral.

In spite of his first inclination to say no, Josh agreed. Dealing with Bianca's cancer, feuding church members, and his general feelings of failure, he didn't think he could offer much support. Josh was spent.

But he walked to the podium anyway.

The final chords of "Go Rest High on That Mountain" wafted into the pores of drywall. The thick scent of florist perfume exaggerated red roses, yellow daisies, pink chrysanthemums, and white baby's breath. Josh rose slowly to preach.

"This isn't Matt lying in the casket." Josh looked at the body, and most of the funeral attendees followed his gaze. "Matt is in paradise today."

As soon as the words left Josh's lips, he felt the surprise sting of jealousy.

"No more pain, no more sorrow, no more death. Jesus has wiped every tear from his eyes." While Josh waited for his comments to sink in, he let his own thoughts wander. He knew he wasn't suicidal, but he did want to die.

He snuck another look at Matt's corpse. He almost felt envious of the peace resting on his face.

"Matt has no more worries of this world. He finished the race set before him. He crossed over to the promised land. Matt's probably checking out his heavenly home right now."

An image appeared in Josh's mind. Shiny streets of gold, the gurgle of crystalline rivers, strong trees laden with emerald-green leaves, and a perfect glow of light cast over it all. Josh wanted to go there.

The family waited for his next words.

"Matt loved his family. Worked with integrity. Cared for the needs of others. And offered practical help whenever it was within his power to do so. Matt fulfilled the role God created exclusively for him. He lived with excellence."

Finished, Josh closed with a prayer, and organ music filled the sanctuary. The funeral directors discreetly guided rows of mourners to the front, where they offered their condolences to Matt's family.

Josh smiled and shook hands with people. But he was not present; he was attending his own funeral. In his head.

What might people say about him? Would his eulogy inspire others to greater endeavors?

At forty-two, Josh didn't know if this was a midlife crisis or just life happening. But he was beat and wanted to check out. If only God would whisk him away to heaven right now. Josh was ready to go.

But God left Josh on earth with his problems.

After months of intensive treatments, Bianca survived her cancer. But they could no longer care for her mother and were forced to place her in a retirement villa.

Harvest Home suffered emotionally, spiritually, and financially from the trauma of the congregational split. And Josh ultimately walked away from the pastorate. He fell prey to the pressures, and his ministry became his message. But it wasn't a message of hope. For him, it was something he'd like to forget.

As managers, we carry a weight of responsibility for those who follow us. Not only does the way we lead affect our survival, but our decisions impact those we work with. If we're not careful, we might back ourselves right into needing a miracle.

Much like Moses, we may not be backed against a brick wall, but we may be pushed against a wall of water. Moses hadn't pursued a position of leadership, and he made many mistakes along the way, but he accepted the role of responsibility. People were screaming and disgruntled, and even his own family was unhappy with his leadership style. And yet, Moses didn't give up—though he surely felt like it.

His actions ultimately saved an entire nation. Depending on Moses's choices, the people trailing behind him would either die or live.

These are the characteristics that made him an irreplaceable manager:

- When things went wrong and he was questioned by his followers, which in turn made him question himself,

FIRST HIRED, LAST FIRED

Moses didn't give up and didn't turn inward. He trusted God for answers, not himself (Exod. 5:17–23).

- Moses dealt with the root of issues. In the face of insubordination and panic, Moses kept a cool head and told the people what was right (Exod. 6:9; 14:10–14).
- Moses accepted the miracle in the problem. Though he was afraid and things looked impossible, based on what God empowered him to do, Moses lifted his hands and led the Israelites forward, toward a new place (Exod. 14:15–22).

Moses didn't always behave with maturity. In his younger years, he too attempted to cover problems, jumped far away from challenges, and thought dealing with an issue once was enough. But he learned from his mistakes. This offers us hope today.

It's never too late to rip bandages off infected wounds where you work. When you overcorrect, rushing from one possible solution to another, and land in the opposite ditch, you can climb out and get back on the highway. Clean communication is always available to refresh mind-sets. It's never too late for a fresh start with fresh faith.

Impulsiveness and avoidance cost money, time, energy, and jobs, while determined discipline, though inconvenient, pays for itself many times over. Josh made mistakes, but he determined to learn from them, and as a result his story turned out much different. Let's watch the miracle unfold.

Joshua Conners flipped the switch, and florescent lights blinked in a succession of ghostly white lights. His 7 A.M. start allowed a morning walk before coming to work.

He couldn't believe how breathing deep of an early dawn energized him. The fingers of God painted new brushstrokes of reds and orange cast against clouds that changed colors as the sun rose higher.

The twitter of birds sang to Josh along the trail. New air, clean and pure. Even his thoughts connected better outdoors.

He felt like a new man—rested and clear headed.

Josh's phone pinged, and he glanced at Ted Foster's text.

"I'll be there."

Now to e-mail Harvest Home's music director and tell him things were arranged. Josh trusted they could reach a workable solution.

After Ted first messaged, Josh called him in and let the older man scrub some of the dirt from his wounds by venting complaints. Then, to further cleanse, Ted and other key members were invited to participate in a brainstorming session. The ground rules were set: no criticizing, no idea too crazy, nothing decided, just thinking out loud.

As the process continued, Ted and those passionate about the music would have a voice in potential changes to the program, but they would not control negatively from the sidelines. Josh would keep an eye on the situation and only involve himself if necessary. Otherwise, the music director and a facilitator would move things forward.

When Josh took the job at Harvest Home, his dreams were naive. He didn't realize how much went on behind the scenes, especially in a growing church. The bigger the congregation, the bigger the challenges. Trying to juggle the wants and needs of so many people was making its mark on Josh's soul. He felt unqualified and inept. That's when the first signs of trouble started.

Josh sat down and carefully pulled the stack of papers toward him. The recent audit committee's findings lay on top. Shortages increased while contributions decreased.

His cell phone rang. Sarah Davis sounded alarmed. "Can you come to the hospital?"

Josh glanced at the full calendar on his computer. "I'll send someone right over. Is anyone with you?"

"The kids are on the way. You can't come?"

Anxiety squeezed Josh's heart. He was torn between his emotions and practicality. He prayed silently, "Show me the wise decision, and give me the courage to act on it."

By the time he opened his eyes, Josh knew how to answer. "I'll come this evening. Hopefully with Bianca. If she's available, my wife gives great hugs." Josh smiled to himself. Lately, he was the happy recipient of a few extra.

He straightened. "In the meantime, I'll make sure you aren't alone."

It only took two calls for Josh to find an available member of their Love in Action team. Rob promised to coordinate care for Sarah and Matt for as long as needed.

With that settled, Josh turned back to the audit report. The multitude of yellow highlights was disconcerting.

Giggling lifted from his secretary's office. Josh looked at his watch: 8:40.

The old knot started.

Last month, Josh had an especially bad episode. He woke up clutching his throat for air, while the four walls tightened around him. The doctor explained that his unresolved frustrations from trying to micromanage were culminating in physical symptoms. Serious ones that could lead to greater illness and early death.

He prescribed delegation, healthier eating, exercise, more sleep, and, as a fellow Christian, intense Bible study on the subject. Moses became Josh's model—a man who found miracles in his problems.

Josh ended up on his knees. "I trust you as the Creator of time and provision to prepare all I need. Help me release the thinking that I must be everyone's problem solver. Forgive me for my arrogance."

Josh's cell interrupted his reflection.

"Be there in five."

Josh pulled out the list he'd started last week. It wouldn't be easy, but he and the newly positioned personnel director would pray over the areas Darlene needed to improve on before talking with her together.

Afterwards, the director would meet with Darlene monthly to mentor her past minor infractions and help guide her to better work habits. The personnel director, a female, would shower her with regular training, expectations, and progress reports. If all efforts failed, then with a panel from the pastoral team, the director would replace Darlene, but only after much prayer and counsel.

But the latter proved unnecessary. Darlene flourished under the new program. It turned out, she simply required better communication, and the personal attentiveness didn't hurt. The personnel director created an atmosphere of accountability, and Darlene grew more confident in her abilities.

For Josh, it relieved one more pressure. He would need that release.

When Bianca's breast cancer diagnosis came, the tragedy pulled the rug out from under their world. But since Josh had already lightened his schedule, there was less chaos. He went to all her treatments, helped more with the kids, and offered greater support. Their marriage was strengthening before this tragedy, but through it they came to adore each other in whole new ways.

The Love in Action team also swooped in and relieved many daily burdens. It didn't escape Josh's attention that heeding the warning signs of his panic attacks and depression enabled the program to exist. Because of his earlier anxiety, their family received immediate care from coordinated members in this crisis.

Josh learned many valuable things through his earlier problems. It wasn't his job to live other people's lives for them. He couldn't allow their burdens to become his. He needed to take care of his own family. And he wasn't the miracle maker; God was.

A few weeks later, Josh was called to preach at a funeral. Before Matt died, Josh visited him in the hospital and at home while he healed from a heart attack. His recovery appeared extraordinary, but then without warning Matt died in his sleep.

The experience freshened how precious time on this earth is. Matt exampled a man who balanced honoring God, caring for his family, and helping others, while maintaining a stunning reputation for his work ethics. The mourning line stretched onto the sidewalk paralleling the city street.

At the service, Josh breathed deep the soothing scent of yellow, blue, red, white, and pink floral arrangements. Behind the podium, he stood to begin the eulogy.

"Men like Matt teach us the value in every situation. To paraphrase Viktor Frankl, life can challenge us to suffer bravely, and yet accepting the challenge gives us meaning until the very end."

Various family members offered soft smiles and nods of encouragement from the front row.

"Matt fulfilled God's plan for him with excellence. He had problems but looked for the opportunity to unwrap the miracle inside each one. He followed God into the promised land."

When the service ended, Josh thought about his own life. Others would follow him, and he had the responsibility to do his best, but he wasn't their savior. He wouldn't try to be. But he would strive to love and care for others—his family first.

Josh stopped fretting and allowed God to show him how to avoid easy outs. Fewer Band-Aids, less ditch-hopping, and more communication showers with those he was authorized to lead. He stopped avoiding and reacting impulsively to challenges. Instead, Josh looked for every opportunity to unwrap the miracle in each problem.

―᭜―

We all make mistakes, but learning from them and looking for the hidden miracle inside the problem can heal and give our lives greater meaning. When we act too quickly, emotional energy drains our physical energy. We risk becoming overdriven, overworked, and overtired. This equation leads to ineffective leadership.

Problems don't go away. Easy outs only cost us in the end—and others pay the price, too.

Moses must have wondered why, when he and the Israelites wandered a barren, dry, hot desert forty years rather than the few weeks it could have taken. But is it possible more time was needed so they didn't miss a greater plan?

The bigger our problem, the bigger our miracle.

But if we rush past our problems, we miss the chance to breathe in those moments of meaning.

Problem solving isn't all about us. When appropriate, addressing problems affecting others also allows us the privilege of being part of their miracle—and makes us irreplaceable. To explore, to risk in unknown areas, to move forward and change the world will bring rewards few ever find.

We'll soon see, great adventures also await those who risk big decisions. It's a mission you won't want to miss.

—————— Investigative Questions ——————

1. Do you ask and trust God for the ability to interpret and solve difficult problems? (Dan. 5:16).

2. Have you considered the ravens, that they do not sow or reap, have no storeroom or barn, and yet God feeds them? Do you know you are much more valuable than birds to him? (Luke 12:24).

3. Do you know the One who is able to do immeasurably more than you ask, or imagine, according to his power at work within us? (Eph. 3:20).

Chapter 10

The Deborah Decision

Adventure is always one yes away.

In our stimulated society, we are bored people.

We are wired for adventure but rarely look at boring situations and ask, "How can I turn this around?"

A select few do.

Change is made by people willing to make change. And yet, change makers almost always face resistance. Therein lies the thrill.

Great leaders introduce revolutionary ideas. And from the beginning, many have been women.

Women who have led people to places they didn't necessarily want to go.

In the twenty-first century, gendered leadership is still a point of contention between men and women. Many men naturally struggle under the guidance of a woman. And at times, so do other women.

Some argue this happens because a woman shouldn't lead; however, this premise isn't biblical. There are examples of women who worked, judged, advised, financed, and held authority over other groups of people, both men and women. Stories sprinkled throughout the Old and New Testaments verify historical accounts of women in charge.

However, women have unique challenges. We aren't always sure of ourselves. We question whether we're out of line, stepping on toes, or usurping another person's position. Even in our day and age, a woman's loyalties are often torn between home and the office. Making the right decision matters to us. Are we aligned with God's will or in opposition to it?

To make things more difficult, if you are a woman called by God to lead others, odds are some of those you supervise will disrespect your directives. And great are the chances they will be unhappy about circumstances they cannot control.

So what do you do, if you are a woman trying to accomplish a job and lead those who would rather do nothing than follow you? Don't focus your attempts on manipulation—turn your energy to positive endeavors. Ask yourself whether you are leading for the right reasons and in the right direction. After prayer, get practical.

Here's a condensed checklist that works for any situation:

- Be someone you'd want to follow. Make wise decisions to do good, not impulsive or petty choices that might harm someone's reputation.
- Reduce TMI. Generally speaking, women share more than the typical man wants to hear. Keep information short, concise, and to the point.
- Don't say, "I have a quick question," or some other lead-in statement. Simply ask your question or make your statement.
- Don't attempt to have two or more conversations at once. Stop trying to talk in person while e-mailing or finishing a phone call. Give the person in front of you the benefit of your full attention.
- Don't say yes or nod your head in agreement unless you are fully engaged in what you heard. If you were distracted

or paying partial attention, be honest and say so. Then apologize and ask the speaker to repeat their request.

- Focus on preventables. There are many things in life and at work we can't control, so let those areas go. Instead, spend time and energy working on preventing problems in areas you can affect.
- Make things smooth for others when possible.
- Don't try to build yourself up or make others look bad. Let your actions represent you.
- Look for invisible drains, and teamwork with others to plug them. Invisible drains are those areas often overlooked or unseen in an organization that sap time, money, energy, or other valuable resources.
- Give credit appropriately, and affirm your appreciation to subordinates publicly. Do this often.

For a more extensive list, please visit my website, www.brooksanita.com. You will also find a copy of a Strategic Leadership Covenant there. This document lists specific biblical characteristics that uniquely identify leaders. Patterns of men and women born for the role.

Sometimes when you're called to authority, it's good to review a black-and-white outline of who you are and who equipped you for the position. Allow God to reveal your unique abilities and calling.

Hailee could have used this kind of reinforcement. Vice president of a moderate-sized insurance agency, she battles a nagging hole in her soul. Hailee's good in the job, but she can't pinpoint what is missing. Let's see if she'll lead herself and others to wake up to a greater destiny—or stay stuck, fighting for a position she both loves and hates.

Hailee unlocked the entrance doors and rushed past two desks to reach her own. The main office of Farmer's Source Insurance Group wouldn't open for Monday's business until eight. Hailee checked her watch, and the time read 7:20 A.M. She was the first one in.

Still, Hailee had hoped to arrive an hour earlier. But her husband was sick, and she needed to make sure he had essentials like Kleenex, water, medicine, and something to eat before leaving the house.

Most of her co-workers were men, with wives who provided support when things got hectic for them. Hailee felt for the wives; many, like her, were busy executives at work and helpmates at home.

Happy to fill the role, but still, lacking something deeper.

Hailee guessed this was the reason the story reported on the morning radio show struck her so hard. Something pierced through a wispy veil over her heart and caused an immediate emotional response. A powerful chill coursed through her veins, ran down her arms, and caused her fingers to twitch as they clutched the steering wheel. Her chin had quivered involuntarily.

She'd never heard anything like the congressman's account, but now Hailee couldn't shake the memory of his horrific story.

Jostling and loud voices filled the room. A steady stream of Farmer's Source agents and office personnel started filing through the front doors.

Hailee turned the computer on and opened her task manager. She hated Monday meetings. Pointless. Hailee despised wasting time.

Within minutes, every desk was occupied with coffee slurping and weekend warrior stories. Hailee rolled her eyes in the middle of Glenn's latest whopper. She moved to a discreet corner in the back of the room and poured boiling water over Samurai Chai tea leaves. The spicy wash over her tongue caused her mind to wander to her sick husband, hoping his taste buds had awakened.

Glenn's booming voice cut off further thought. No wonder he was their top selling agent. You couldn't ignore him. "Bases were loaded, the pitcher threw it dead center, and as soon as my bat connected with the ball, I knew it. I'd hit the sweet spot. Grand slam."

"Win the game?" Jerry said.

"Nah, still lost by two. Next inning, Joey headed for a steal but questioned himself halfway through. He had a clear shot but lost confidence. Once he hesitated, the second baseman picked him off before he could get back to first."

Hailee scowled and thought, "Don't these guys ever think of anything but sports?"

Cal made his way to the front of the room. His teeth sparkled from a recent whitening, made more drastic against his darkly tanned skin.

"How was Cancun?" Glenn called out with a wink.

Cal scanned his audience. "Fantastic. The weather was perfect, our hotel was top rate, and the beaches were full of . . . , ahem," Cal's gaze met Hailee's. "The beaches were full of interesting people."

Hailee offered Cal a slight nod of approval for changing descriptions. She knew if there were no women in the room, the play-by-play would sound very different. She wondered what he would think of the radio program this morning?

Cal tapped his coffee cup for attention and finally started. "Let's settle down." He made his way to the back of the office where Hailee had prepared a dry-erase board with a blank template. All he had to do was fill in the figures. "First, quarterly sales reports."

Glenn, now perched haphazardly on the edge of Hailee's desk, slung his leg back and forth while he spouted figures.

Cal scratched numbers in the blanks.

Same scenario, different day. The air of monotony smothered Hailee.

"What about our commercial accounts?" Cal turned his attention to Kate, the southwest regional sales manager.

Kate's shoulders slumped. "We're down 6 percent from last quarter. Since Global Mutual hit our region, we're taking a pretty good hit."

The statement struck Cal's most sensitive nerve. Money. There was no missing the passion in his question. "What are we doing about it?"

Cricket quiet answered the question rebounding off the walls.

Hailee squirmed, but at least the conflict added some sizzle to the room.

Cal, all business now, broke the silence. "I know you guys are smarter than this. Someone better speak. Why are we losing clients to our competitor?"

Words burst from every direction. Each shouting over the others. Everyone seemed to have an opinion on the problems but no solutions. Disputes broke out over the reasons their commercial clientele was leaving.

Hailee shook her head in frustration. Cal would get everyone stirred up, but little would change. The tension ball at the base of her skull swelled.

When the meeting adjourned, nothing had changed, except added pressure among the agents. Hailee yawned while she waited for Glenn to finish schmoozing Cal. If he was sincere it wouldn't bother her, but Glenn didn't breathe without a motive.

"We haven't had an incentive program lately. Might spur sales. Maybe cash plus a Caribbean cruise? One of those sandy beaches you were talking about. Say, for the sales leader over the next two quarters?" Glenn winked at his boss.

Hailee partially admired Glenn's boldness, even while his saccharine-sweet methods made her skin crawl. She unleashed her frustration. "And of course you would take your name out of the hat. Wouldn't want anyone to think you were being selfish, now would we?"

Hatred shot from Glenn's gray eyes before they softened and shifted in Cal's direction. "A little competition's a good thing."

Hailee balled her fists. "That bonus money you're talking about could help someone besides yourself."

"Down, tiger."

"Quit making everything about you."

"Who are you to judge?"

Cal's lips thinned. "All right, you two. This isn't getting us anywhere." He looked from one to the other. "I don't care who takes charge, I just want to sell more commercial lines."

Hailee felt the implied threat in Cal's interjection.

Glenn backed up. "You're right. I'll get on it—no time like the present." He fumbled in his pocket for keys. "As a matter of fact, I have an appointment with a client in less than an hour." He scowled at Hailee then escaped out the door.

Hailee considered telling Cal about her idea. The one that sprouted from the radio broadcast.

But the voice in her head started talking first.

It's stupid. Cal will think you've lost your mind. You need to focus your energies on your career goals instead of on something that won't equate to a crumb on the table.

Glenn's laughing face popped into her mind.

Like a jealous child, Hailee turned on her competitive edge. "Look, Cal, Glenn's weak when it comes to follow-through. I'll have to be the one to strengthen our commercial client relationships, or it won't get done."

Cal's eyes appeared glazed over, and his only response was a nod.

Hailee knew better than to play Glenn's game.

It was clear Cal wasn't really paying attention. The fact was confirmed when he excused himself and left Hailee standing alone. True to character, Cal breezed out of the office to play golf.

Hailee grumbled and went to her desk.

She dialed the first number. "Mr. Martin, this is Hailee. From Farmer's Source Insurance?"

"What can I do for you?" The invitation didn't sound sincere.

"I hate to bother you, but I have a quick question."

"I'm busy right now."

"If you'll allow me a few minutes, I'll explain."

"Sorry, I don't have time to talk."

"But..." the phone's life line buzzed flat. Mr. Martin had hung up.

A thick crust hardened around Hailee's emotions, and she plunged into making more calls. Through persistence, she managed to snag a few appointments with potential clients.

Hailee marched through the task, bored and frustrated.

At lunch, she didn't intend to, but Hailee took her jaded attitude out on her sick husband. He had no way of knowing what was gnawing her insides. She wasn't a very good nurse during those couple days of recovery. About the amount of time it took for her to push the last vestiges of that silly idea out of her mind.

In the following months, Hailee's resentment grew. The people she worked with cared for nothing but making money and looking out for number one. Feeling defeated, she joined their crowd.

In the meantime, Global Mutual marched deeper into Farmer Source's territory. Hailee made surface attempts to build a stronger commercial base, but she lacked true passion for the project.

In a matter of months, Cal flew in from a trip to the Virgin Islands and announced an accelerated cost-cutting plan. Several jobs were eliminated before the end of the year.

Even Glenn's demise didn't make Hailee feel like she'd won anything. She had mixed feelings about retaining hers.

Cal refocused the company, with an emphasis on a leaner enterprise. Farmer's Source Insurance survived but without the thrill of victory.

Hailee blamed her boredom on a lack of solid leadership from Cal. The company's weariness was contagious. She stayed because her paycheck put food on the table. But with each day that passed, another piece of Hailee withered, while she struggled to figure out why.

In today's economic climate, many of us place our hope in others. Maybe the government can save us. Big corporations should do something. We grouse when no one steps up with a fast fix.

But what if you were the one who was supposed to act? Are you waiting for someone else to begin the adventure you are meant to lead? Are your ideas lying dormant because you're afraid to speak up? Can a woman really make decisions men will follow?

In the book of Judges, a woman named Deborah led the entire nation of Israel. During a time of great turmoil, she proved savvy, smart, and decisive when the situation called for important action. And yet, Deborah did not try to usurp men; instead, she guided them to a tactical conclusion. Deborah offered personal support and wise advice, while taking nothing from her counterparts.

She wasn't afraid to venture into unknown territories and seize opportunities when they became available.

Deborah's strategy provides a clear map for powerful leadership today.

- Deborah avoided a central role in conflicts. She helped decide disputes in a nonthreatening environment (Judg. 4:4–5).
- When God directed her words, Deborah spoke with confidence and bravery (Judg. 4:6–7).
- In the face of cowardice, Deborah did not waste time pointing it out. She did not try to stand in the way of natural consequences of the poor choices of others. She supported the person, even if she disagreed with the decision (Judg. 4:8–10).
- When the battle was won, Deborah didn't point to herself. She gave credit first to God, and then to those who worked with her (Judg. 5).

Making an initial decision is often the hardest step we take. But irreplaceable employees make sound choices and stick to them. They don't waffle back and forth, wondering whether they did the right thing. They have confidence in their fact gathering and in wise counsel, and they show grace while they implement strategic practices.

Through an everyday circumstance, Hailee became aware of an important need. She turned her boredom upside down, explored possibilities, and discovered an adventurous endeavor. By looking at Deborah's battle plan, Hailee mapped her own tactics for victory. She unlocked her destiny and freed others in response.

———

Hailee listened to the morning show while she waited for the light to turn green.

Dusty, Clear Channel's radio personality, introduced his guest, Congressman Chase Hall. "Thank you for talking to us about this sensitive issue. The statistics are startling."

The congressman cleared his throat. "Every year as many as 17,500 people are trafficked to the United States from over fifty countries around the world. Eighty percent are female and fifty percent are children. And I believe these are conservative figures."

"Kids are trafficked into the U.S.?"

"Absolutely. Thailand, Mexico, Philippines, Haiti, India, Guatemala, and the Dominican Republic are all countries identified as origins for domestic human trafficking into America."

"How do they get away with this?" Dusty sounded alarmed.

"Thousands of children are trafficked annually into urban centers such as Washington, DC, New York, St. Louis, Atlanta, and Los Angeles. Tourist locations such as Las Vegas and Florida are also major destinations for human trafficking victims."[4]

"Why tourist centers?"

"The urban connection is twofold. The obvious reason is the ease with which you can lose people in metropolitan areas. But what few people realize is that major events like conventions and sports tournaments draw demands from wealthy predators. They have the money and the means to feed their sick appetites."

The Deborah Decision

The light turned green, and Hailee eased into a turn she'd made hundreds of times before. But she didn't notice; her mind was fixed on the men on the radio.

"So what are you trying to accomplish by speaking out?"

"I hope others will join me in the fight to rescue these modern-day slaves. But their freedom isn't enough. These women and children require assistance to acclimate. Not only are most of them terrified, thrust into a strange land, where American customs are totally foreign, but they have no resources to adjust. On top of that, they've been brainwashed through starvation, drugs, and beatings and are conditioned to fear people under daily doses of horrific mental abuse. This is a growing epidemic. They're human beings and deserve to be set free."

"Amen," Dusty shouted, while a round of enthusiastic clapping ended the program.

Hailee didn't know why the echo of this story was causing a flood of instantaneous adrenaline to flow through her body. Her muscles tensed, and her breath fluttered. She'd never heard anything like it before, and yet it felt as if she were personally connected to the women and children who were hurting.

Her imagination created scenes of dark torture chambers, where girls and boys huddled in hunger and terror. Noticeable bruises would not be acceptable, as these children would need to please paying vultures. The thought made her feel like vomiting on the side of the road.

The rest of the drive Hailee talked with herself. She replayed the report in her mind repeatedly. The percentages burned her brain.

Someone needed to do something.

The congressman's final sentence boomeranged in her head. "They're human beings and deserve to be set free."

Hailee pulled into the parking lot at Farmer's Source Insurance. She turned off the ignition and spoke to the woman in the mirror. "They deserve to know there are people who genuinely care."

183

Fresh from her intense study of Deborah over the weekend, Hailee wondered what the prophet would have thought about mixing ancient practices with modern technology to combat the problem. She dictated a few notes into her phone. Tactics Map, Soldiers, Officers, Allies, Enemies, Defensive Weapons, Offensive Weapons, Debriefing.

Throughout the agency meeting, Hailee couldn't help zoning out. If her husband hadn't gotten sick, she never would have heard Dusty on the radio. Without that experience, this new stirring wouldn't make her feel more alive than she had in years.

Farmer's Source Insurance Group could help fulfill a greater mission, and Hailee had an idea on a strategy to get them there. She had to try.

Periodically, waves of doubt would topple her growing excitement. One moment she felt confidence, and the next it felt like the dumbest idea in the history of mankind.

When the meeting ended, Hailee walked cautiously up on a conversation between Glenn and Cal. On the cusp of her others-focused thoughts, Glenn's self-serving request grated her nerve.

How can he think about Caribbean vacations when children and women are being tortured?

Hailee took a deep breath and curbed her impulse to react out of emotions. She needed to catch Cal before he ran off. Using slow, clear, concise words, she spoke. "Cal, can I talk to you for a few minutes?"

Glenn glowered. "Do you mind? We're in the middle of a conversation."

Hailee narrowed her thoughts to Deborah's intentional avoidance of conflict. The female leader of Israel made decisions and exercised them with boldness and bravery.

Hailee offered Glenn a pensive smile. "If this wasn't of the utmost importance, I wouldn't interrupt. Please forgive me, Glenn. I promise to keep it short. And I'd like to talk with you about this later. Your involvement could make a crucial difference."

"Can't wait." Glenn ducked his head in a mock bow but, after Cal gave him a shoulder shrug, complied with Hailee's request by walking away.

Hailee didn't waste any time. She laid out the initial shell of her strategy. It took effort to quell the excitement in her passionate plea. Hundreds of unknown souls needed rescue.

"We are primed to do something. We have good people, the right connections, and it would help our reputation." She took a quick gulp of air. "You have a twelve-year-old daughter. How you would feel if someone stole her off a beach while you were on vacation and threw her into a foreign country to traffic?"

Riveted, Cal drew her to a seated position at the closest desk.

He pulled another chair across from her and sat down. "Go on." Cal cracked his knuckles but didn't break eye contact.

Hailee's vision expanded the more she talked.

Cal interrupted, "We're not equipped to take on something of this magnitude."

"Leave the details to me."

Cal leaned forward on his elbows. "Like what?"

"I think several corporate clients would clamor to get involved. I want to be clear, though; the motive is not to develop relationships so we can get their business. If it happens naturally, then fine, but this project requires purity."

"Agreed." Cal rubbed his index finger against his temple in contemplation.

"It's a lot to absorb, but together, we can wipe out this atrocity."

"Down, general. Let's not cross into battle too quick."

A bit embarrassed, Hailee lowered her chin. But thinking of Deborah, she lifted her eyes to square her gaze against Cal's. "Every few seconds, another child endures untold pain at the hands of men who purchase them like livestock. With your permission, I'd like to talk with our troops tomorrow."

"Sounds like you're a woman with a plan. I'm not sure this will work, but I'll trust you to lead the way." Cal glanced at his watch. "I'm late for my golf game."

Hailee rushed home at lunch to doctor her husband and tell him her story. His cautious advice helped her take a step back and adjust her approach.

Back at work, she sent a group e-mail, inviting all Farmer's Source employees to the next day's rally. She said just enough to raise curiosity.

Next, she created a spreadsheet with a list of commercial clients in the area who might partner. She dialed the president of Jones Pharmaceutical first.

Mr. Martin answered on the second ring.

"I have a proposition you won't want to miss."

"Who is this?" Mr. Martin questioned.

"Hailee Aden from Farmer's Source Insurance."

"I have enough insurance."

"I'm not selling policies, I'm offering you a chance to be part of something bigger than yourself. To save lives."

"How's that?"

It only took thirty minutes for Mr. Martin to support Hailee's vision.

She signed four more commitments to the cause before going home. Hailee practically skipped to her car.

She stayed up most of the night preparing materials.

The next morning, Hailee wheeled into her usual parking spot. She lifted her eyes to the sky and prayed for wisdom and guidance, then got out and walked to the passenger side.

She hauled flip charts, a black portfolio case, and a red book bag to the front entrance. Then dropped her cargo on the ground in order to unlock the door.

The rising sun reflected off the large, white rectangular pages. She squinted and managed to get everything under her arms, so she could hoist it inside. With relief, Hailee mounded the objects on top of her desk.

At the back of the office, she dusted the easel off and set the pre-written pages on the stand. Next, she pulled a large plastic baggie full of rainbow-hued markers from the book bag and staged them close to the chart. Hailee then slid a hand-drawn map of each manager's region from the portfolio and taped them on the walls behind the flip chart.

She stacked blank Post-it notes next to the markers and finally added a checklist she'd written at home. They would brainstorm off these triggers.

- Who's impacted? Every business, industry, and region touched directly or indirectly. Who has children? Grandchildren?
- Identify all possible clues. Transportation, food, banking, lodging facilities, clothing.
- Map backwards. Radiate from the end to the beginning. Use Post-it notes to thread parts of the process together. (This way you can move things around to ensure steps are placed in correct order and nothing is missed.)
- Continue mapping backwards until you arrive at the origin. The kidnapping, brainwashing, or manipulation that brought them to America.

Hailee was sipping a fresh cup of chai tea when Glenn entered the office almost forty-five minutes later.

"Whoa, what happened in here?" Glenn walked to the back wall and feathered his left hand across one of the map layouts.

Hailee didn't know why she suddenly felt bashful, but Glenn's comment made her feel exposed, vulnerable. "Just something I put together to help us design a game plan for this project. I'm glad you got here first; I'd like to tell you how you can help."

Glenn grunted, "Looks like we're going to war."

"Kind of."

He crossed his arms over his chest.

With heart pounding and nerves jumping, Hailee began. "Your sales skills could save lives."

"I don't think selling insurance ever saved anyone. Might help the family members though." Glenn laughed at his own morbid joke.

"Not directly, but if you'll hear me out, I think I can show you can save someone from a slow death."

Glenn listened but wasn't convinced. "I'm not sure I want to take on dangerous types. Sounds crazy to me."

"We aren't acting as law enforcement. That's a job for professionals. But we can lead these boys and girls back to life after near death." She took a slow breath. "Burying our heads won't make it go away. Doing nothing is doing something. This is war."

The room erupted with new voices. Glenn scuttled away.

She let them get settled, then Hailee used her hands to shush the group. "Please, everyone, we've got a lot to cover. I'm going to tell you about something difficult, and yet I think if we put our heads together we can do something about it. We have the opportunity to step out of our so-so lives and do something exciting."

Cal slipped in the door and leaned against a side wall. He smiled and nodded encouragement.

With an hour allocated, the energy in the room elevated to an excited frenzy by the ticking of the final minutes. Many added their insights to the vision.

Afterward, those committed to the cause dedicated two hours per week and started the war. Cal was one of them. Weekly planning sessions, strategic partnerships, and tactical moves helped them march closer, all led by Hailee.

Over several months, the commercial side of their insurance business naturally grew when word got out about their project. And Farmer's reputation for integrity and humanitarian efforts landed them several awards.

Through constant encouragement, Hailee garnered a network of allies in the effort. In less than three years, they gave fifty-two children a soft place to land in eight survivor safe havens. They called them Farmer Houses.

Before long, other professionals requested Hailee's services as a consultant. She accepted numerous engagements but pointed their accolades to God and the legion of people who'd worked on the program.

Thanks to one woman's decision, a group of employees at a regional insurance agency lived an amazing adventure. They turned their company into the largest in the southwest. But, more important, they'd become part of something greater than themselves.

Hailee took them into a battle the men might have overlooked, where they saved lives and set people free. Boredom was no longer an issue.

Embracing the unknown is a scary proposition, but the risk could change us and others for a greater good. Human beings are designed to make a difference, but a decision must be made first. A decision to say yes.

In small or big ways, you are meant to take action that changes the world around you. It's why you exist. Otherwise, boredom sets in. To succeed in fulfilling your purpose is to succeed in every aspect of being. The uniqueness of your gender, personality, or style may equip you for something special. A way to offer hope to others.

But action out of balance is exhaustive. As we'll see next, having the energy to do great things rests solely on how you treat yourself. The good news is, a wellness plan was written before you were ever born.

——————— Investigative Questions ———————

1. Do you merely listen to the word and deceive yourself? Or do what it says? (James 1:22).

2. Are you ready to accept what no eye has seen, no ear has heard, and no human mind has conceived? The things God has prepared out of love for you? (1 Cor. 2:9).

3. When you decide what will be done, do you have confidence that God will shine light on your ways? (Job 22:28).

Chapter 11

The Jethro Joust

Just because you can,
doesn't mean you should.

The temptation to write seven days a week was powerful while I finished this book. Especially since the publisher's contract called for me to complete it during the peak part of our river resort season. As a leader, my work hours are long.

Yet, even during my busiest time of year, I take a Sabbath rest.

I've attended and spoken at many business conferences. Inevitably, one question from owners and managers in business of all sizes crops up. "How do I run a successful business and still have time for a life?"

The answer is simple, but not necessarily easy.

Make the choice to take a break. It's a decision.

When you do this, know you must allow those filling in to do the job—without trying to control every minute detail from a distance.

Realize it's possible to reach the same destination from a different direction. Let others do their best to help you, then turn the tables and make sure you offer them a break.

You have permission to rest. To take physical and mental breaks from work. For millennia, the ancient text of the Bible has told us to let our bodies and minds wind down. It's the healthy thing to do. Even God rested.

The Bible has much to say about the importance of a twenty-four hour break from everyday activities. And it clashes with the message we receive from the world.

In our rushed culture, we are made to feel guilty if we don't work ourselves into an early grave. Prodded and pushed by conveniences like smartphones, tablets, laptops, and online everything. We are given no excuse for reprieve.

And there's an additional negative side effect. Without a mental and emotional break from work, we lose joy. Exhaustion translates into a broken fun meter. Nothing steals our joy like fatigue.

What about you? Are you too tired to laugh? When was the last time you let loose with a belly, giggle, snort, genuine let-it-all-go laugh? If you can't remember laughter, then how about your last heartfelt smile? Can you recall breathing in the joy of living?

For the first time in history, we live in a warp-speed society where every human being is expected to make themselves available 24/7/365. The pressure to perform squeezes the life and laughter out of us.

Each new project pushes us closer to a mental and emotional edge. We start out energized, creative, and highly productive. But, without a break, the wear on our bodies and minds throws us into a spinning mass of exhaustion. Without taking the time to refresh, we chase ever-elusive feel-goods until we can't go anymore.

Finally, we plunge into an abyss of mind-numbing movement, but in reality we're going through the motions. We might appear okay on the surface, but deep inside the truth of our exhaustive efforts takes its toll.

We wake up one morning and realize our relationships are broken. We no longer know how to relax and enjoy ourselves. Our fun meters need repair, and we're too tired to fix them. People begin to avoid us because no one likes the attitude of a tired person. Sometimes, we're the last to realize we've become a Negative Ned.

Busyness magnifies burnout. Until maintaining an irreplaceable position at work is the last thing on our minds.

Those who follow our lead lack direction and are confused by the change in focus. Making a difference no longer matters.

Mike, pushed beyond his own physical and mental abilities, struggled under a weight of his own making. He no longer felt as if he had something to look forward to. The busyness that used to drive him drove him over the edge. With catastrophic consequences.

———

The alarm screamed, and Mike flailed to slam the button. He stretched and groaned at the dull throb deep inside his body. Sharp tingles vibrated through his muscles. Though he slept almost seven hours, Mike could feel a cranky cloud pressing on him, yet he couldn't pinpoint why.

His wife, Melanie, rolled and mumbled in her sleep.

Used to pushing through pain, Mike groaned as he made himself vault from the bed. But this time, Mike couldn't stop the drumbeat in the sinews of his muscle tissue. Something felt different.

Still half asleep, Mike stumbled in to shave. The burning scent of aftershave penetrated his nostrils and nudged his senses awake. He was still patting his jawline when he noticed a distinctive twitch above his right eye. Now what?

Mike rubbed the extra fog off the mirror, leaned close, brushed his graying brown hair back, then used his thumb and forefinger to prop his right eye open. But he saw nothing besides the typical bloodshot white around a gray-blue pupil.

"What's wrong?"

Mike jumped in surprise at his wife's voice. He dropped his hand and turned to look at her. "My eye's twitching, and I can't figure out what's causing it."

"Let me see." She prodded for a few seconds. Just as she pulled her fingers back, Mike's right brow jumped. "It's the nerve above your eye. Probably from working yourself to death."

Mike let out an exasperated sigh. "Don't start on me again."

"Excuse me for caring." Melanie turned and left for the kitchen.

Mike wavered between feeling bad and succumbing to his edgy attitude. Melanie meant well, but the last thing he needed was her hovering over him. He was fine. And he certainly didn't want to be babied. His cranky side won.

Without meaning to, he bit Melanie's head off when she offered a quick breakfast. "I'll drive through Starbucks."

"Suit yourself." Like so many recent mornings, she'd buried her face in a devotional book, while he rushed to the door. Melanie barely looked up when he groused a quick good-bye on his way out. There was no peck on the cheek.

Mike washed his ham and cheese down with a grande Pike Place roast. The coffee helped but didn't totally mask his weariness.

Even when he crossed the threshold of Myriad Marketing, he didn't get the familiar surge of adrenaline he expected. Mike had always counted on his adrenal glands to provide the burst of power necessary to launch him through. But today, even they seemed to rebel.

He muddled through the morning routine. Employees came and went with requests and demands like bees coming and going inside a busy hive. Reports needed review and required signatures. E-mails called from his in-box. Meetings were held, and important decisions made, but as president of the company, Mike was unusually quiet.

He assumed his poor attention and feeble energy weren't visible on the outside. No one seemed to notice his lethargic state.

By two, Mike felt like his head had been slammed inside a microwave. He threw three ibuprofen back in a gulp of Diet Coke. The tension crunching his neck radiated into his shoulders. He glanced at his watch. Roberts was waiting on him to oversee the campaign for Apple's latest technological advance, Legacy.

Mike curled his mouth into a grimace and pushed away from the desk. No one was going to do the job for him.

It took little time for Mike to see the campaign wasn't refined. He interrupted the professionally dressed woman midpresentation. "You haven't thought this through."

"But, I haven't gotten to . . ."

Mike cut her off. "I know what you're going to tell me. But I don't want to hear the excuses. Your team needs to put more time and thought into this project. I expect better and want to see a transformed campaign by 9 A.M. Monday."

"This Monday?" The woman looked nervously at her cohorts.

"Is working through the weekend an issue for you?" Mike challenged the group with a single sweep around the room.

No one dared question his ability to force the issue. Mike nodded in agreement as if they had all said yes to his demand. He left them scrambling to start over.

By five thirty, Mike was back at his desk. He'd be lucky if he made it home before nine. At least Melanie didn't harp about his late work nights anymore. She knew he'd order Chinese or a pizza to get by. He assumed she'd eat with one of her friends or alone with one of her books, since their children were raised and gone.

Mike was fielding a barrage of employee complaints from a meltdown in the graphics department when his cell phone rang. He was surprised to see Russell's name on the display. The CEO, and Mike's mentor, rarely called beyond three in the afternoon. After a heart attack five years ago, Russell had redefined his priorities. Working late didn't fit into the equation.

"This is a pleasant surprise." Mike massaged his neck as he spoke.

"Still micromanaging?"

The remark added a splinter to Mike's stinging shoulders. He forced a chuckle from his throat, but there was no emotion to back it up. "The work won't finish itself. Besides, apparently our employees need a glorified babysitter."

"You sound especially low today. What's going on?"

"Nothing I can't handle. The usual for a Friday. Squabbling in our graphics team, the Legacy campaign needs refinement before we present, and my in-box overfloweth. Just another day."

"I'm concerned about you, Mike. Your body and soul can only be pushed so far."

The leather on Mike's chair squeaked as he wriggled. "Do you mind if we have this conversation another time? I'm never going to get out of here if I don't get back to work."

"Ignoring the situation won't make it go away. I've been where you are, and I don't want you to end up where I landed."

"I appreciate your concern, but I've got things under control. I'll call you next week. We should have the Legacy thing wrapped up then. We can have you over for dinner."

"I'll be waiting for that call."

"Sure thing. I'll talk to you later."

Mike staved off his exhaustion through sheer will until nine forty-five. Then his drooping lids refused to cooperate. He drove home in a daze, nearly nodding off behind the wheel more than once.

At home, he muttered a greeting to Melanie, slipped into pajamas, and dropped in bed. He tossed over problems at the office. Sometime in the throes of night, he drifted into anxious sleep.

The next coherent thought Mike had came from his mental profanity directed at the wailing alarm. Just like the previous morning, he cringed at the heavy weights pushing painfully against his muscles.

It took three tries before he could leverage off the bed.

Melanie squirmed. "It's the weekend. Why don't you stay in and get some rest?"

"I can't."

She propped herself up on an elbow and cocked an eyebrow. "You're the boss."

"There are too many people counting on me."

"Surely there are others who can help lighten your load."

"It's my responsibility."

"Fine." Melanie rolled so her back faced her husband. She scrunched the pillow tight around her head and rattled her lips like a horse.

Mike stared at her balled-up outline, silky brunette strands peeking around the pillow. Even like this, he missed his wife. But he couldn't let himself think about it now. He left the room and got ready for another day.

His footsteps echoed under the vaulted ceilings of Myriad Marketing. Without the bustle of weekday activity, silence clung to the walls; an air of stillness prevailed, as if the building stood alone amid a nuclear wasteland.

Mike shook dark thoughts back to their corners and made his way to the office. He used to feel a thrill at having the place to himself. The excitement of uninterrupted productive hours charged him with vigor. Eons ago.

Still, Mike appreciated the absence of ringing phones, door knocks, scraping easels, and clicking keyboards. And though he still felt tired, at least he was able to cover a lot of detail in his nine hours. He could finish the rest tomorrow.

In a celebratory mood, he called Melanie. "I'm getting ready to leave. How about dinner out tonight? Someplace nice?"

"You're leaving before six?"

"All right, Missy, do you want to go or not?"

She giggled, "You haven't called me Missy in a while." With a touch of flirtation to her voice, she added, "I think I'd love to."

The atmosphere at Favanelle lightened both of their outlooks. Over candlelight, they sipped their drinks, cooled by clinking ice. The conversation remained unusually light, centered on kids and grand-kids. Until dessert.

"Russell called me today," Melanie said.

Mike thought her tone sounded too casual. He pared a chunk of cheesecake with his fork before answering. "Oh? What did he have to say?"

"He's worried."

Mike let his cake-laden fork clatter against the dessert plate. Several heads turned toward their table. He lowered his head and hissed, "Can't we have a pleasant night without your nagging?"

Tears gathered quickly in round ponds at the edges of Melanie's eyes. "I'm not nagging. I'm only telling you what Russell said."

Mike lifted his head and leaned back in the chair. In a careful, calculated, and quiet voice, he said, "You're both making something out of nothing. I'm fine."

"We haven't taken a vacation since the kids moved out."

"Let me catch up, and I'll take you anywhere you want to go."

"You'll never catch up."

Mike picked up his fork and swallowed the cheesecake without tasting it. "Why would I want to spend a vacation with that attitude?"

The ponds channeled onto Melanie's cheeks. Her brown eyes glistened. "You always twist things and make it my fault."

"I don't want to fight with you."

"Neither do I, but at least when we fight, you talk to me."

"I can't win." He threw his napkin on his plate.

"Come to church with me tomorrow." Melanie's change in subject caught Mike off guard.

He felt a flush spread across the center of his face. "I can't. Maybe next week."

"Can't you take one day off? Why don't you go to church and spend the rest of your day relaxing with your family, like a normal person?"

"You're out of touch. That's an old-fashioned normal. None of the people I know take a whole day off. Not the ones who want to stay ahead. Those ideas flew out the window with computers."

"Maybe that's what's wrong with this world."

Mike squirmed. After his heart attack, Russell said things like that.

Melanie had little to say on the drive home or the next morning as she dressed for church. Mike got ready for the office. More and more, it felt like they lived separate lives. Mike really did love his wife.

He forced her out of his mind the rest of the day.

The silvery moon was high in the late night sky when Mike came home. There was no goodnight kiss after he crawled in bed.

Monday morning, Mike woke up feeling a bit like Bill Murray in *Groundhog Day*. He slapped at the alarm and fought his exhausted cloud and clumsy muscles.

Melanie was still upset from Saturday night, so he didn't bother with morning pleasantries before walking out the door.

He drove his patterned route to work. Mike was midway through a left turn on Vine Street, when his arm seized and locked. Fear as tight as the uncontrollable grip on his body latched his thoughts.

Mike started yelling out loud at his own limbs. "Move, I said move," but they staunchly disobeyed. A paralyzing numbness snaked past his elbow. Panic smothered plain fear.

Without warning, a pile-driving headache slammed inside his skull. Then a pressure like nothing he'd ever experienced seemed to press at every cell in his 5'9" frame.

Mike didn't see the car. By the time it T-boned him, his eyesight had pitched black. He never woke up.

Mike's death shocked everyone at Myriad Marketing, but though it was shaky, the company moved on without him. A replacement was quickly moved into position, with little time to adjust.

It was worse for his family. Mike had missed the chance to say a final "I love you" to Melanie. He didn't get to tell his children and grandchildren good-bye. When Mike left the earth, his strongest relationship was with his work.

———

Mike made the mistake so many of us are making today. We allow adrenal overload to push us beyond the limits of God's design for the human body. It's a plague ravaging our planet. This epidemic is especially invasive in Westernized cultures that push people to feed off their work. We treat people like they're worthless if they desire rest. And yet our bodies were created with a need to rejuvenate.

If we adhere to a plan for rest, not only can we do more, but we do it better. It takes more than a good sleep one night a week; it takes consistent patterns of healing rest. Refusing to listen to our bodies results in a pervasive weariness cloaking our best, inside and out. Our greatest potential is missed when we try to work from a weakened state.

We were designed with a requirement for an allocated day of rest. The human body needs time set aside to rejoice when our batteries run low.

We're a society drowning in activities, yet we lack a sense of accomplishment and constantly feel behind. Breathless in a sleep-deprived state, the symptoms of overrun schedules take their toll, and, though we run faster, we produce less. Most workers operate in a state of constant fatigue. If they slow down long enough to notice, they feel helpless to regain their strength. Leaders, in particular, are pressured to do more in less time. In our desire to save money, we push too hard. The results cost us and the organizations we represent.

A perpetual state of fatigue is not the plan our loving God laid out for us. And it won't provide optimal health. We can temporarily push past our intended limits, but it doesn't take long for exhaustion to catch up with us. Sometimes with dire results.

In the book of Exodus, Jethro recognized in Moses the signs of a man managing too much. He mentored his son-in-law to rest up, utilize the abilities of others, and stop wearing himself out so he could produce more.

- Jethro took notice of the heavy burden Moses carried from trying to do everything alone (Exod. 18:13–14).
- Jethro rebuked Moses with a reality check. He used reason and common sense to point out that Moses would wear himself out, because the burden was too heavy. He wisely said it was too much for one man (Exod. 18:15–18).
- Jethro did not tell Moses to quit everything. He pointed out the roles Moses should fill as the ultimate leader of the nation (Exod. 18:19–20).

- A detailed selection process was outlined by Jethro to ensure Moses didn't throw just any warm body into a job. The importance of the assignment required special delegation (Exod. 18:21).
- According to Jethro, once the delegates had weeded out the minor cases, those of highest importance should be brought to Moses. In this way, Jethro offers the first example of teamwork on the job (Exod. 18:22).
- By doing this as God directed, Jethro promised Moses and all the people would go home satisfied when the work was finished (Exod. 18:23).

Jethro wisely instructed Moses to stop trying to do everything himself. Even though his intentions were good.

Most of us don't aspire to become workaholics. But, as with many things that aren't good for us, bad habits slip in before we know it. If we're blessed, God will send someone like Jethro along with a strong and true rebuke. His admonition to pursue God's solution of delegation enabled Moses to rest from his weariness.

Mike was given the same opportunity. The key was whether he'd listen or not.

The buzzing alarm seemed to vibrate through Mike's entire body. He grumbled as he pushed both palms off the mattress to force himself into a standing position. It started in the shower, and, by the time he dried off, he couldn't ignore the twitch above his right eye.

Melanie didn't help matters with her dig about working too hard. But these days they didn't have much else to talk about.

The tired ache followed Mike into Myriad Marketing. Still, he powered on, hiding his fatigue under a snappish exterior. The Legacy campaign team caught his heat when he demanded they work through the weekend to improve their presentation.

By the time Russell called at five thirty, some of the employees had escaped to start their weekend, at least the ones able to avoid Mike's watchful eye.

"This is a pleasant surprise." Mike tried to massage the knots from his neck.

"Still micromanaging?"

Mike bristled at his friend and mentor's pointed comment. He sighed into the telephone. "Someone has to babysit."

"You sound especially jaded today."

"Nothing I can't handle. We've got a few glitches and bickering among employees. The usual for a Friday."

"You're tackling too much. Delegate."

"Do you mind if we have this conversation another time?"

"Ignoring the situation won't make it go away."

"I appreciate your concern, but I've got things under control. I'll call you next week."

"This won't go away."

"I'll talk to you later." Mike pushed his end button.

Mike worked later than he planned and nearly crashed twice on his way home. Once inside, he nodded at Melanie as he stumbled toward their bed.

But he couldn't sleep. He tossed side to side. Unable to disregard the office problems swirling inside his head, he got up for a glass of water. On his way back to the bed, Mike spotted Melanie's devotional book on her bedside table.

The binding cracked as he fanned the pages apart. He flipped through until he came to the current date. What he read astounded him.

The short story described a man like him, and the Bible verse at the bottom referred to a passage in Exodus 18. Mike started opening drawers in the nightstand. In exasperation, he got out of bed.

When he looked up, Melanie stood in the doorway. "What are you doing?"

"Looking for a Bible."

"A what?" his wife's eyes widened.

"You heard me. Where's it at?"

Melanie crossed her arms over her chest.

Mike blew out an exasperated breath. "Can you hurry? I want to read something."

"Certainly, oh mighty king." She dropped in a fake curtsy before leaving the room. A giggle trailed behind her.

When Melanie finally handed him the heavy book, Mike shuffled through the tissuey pages in the front. Then he stabbed the page he was looking for.

With a racing index finger tracing the passage, Mike mumbled the Scriptures as he read. Then he read the entire thing again. Melanie stood near the bed looking puzzled while he scanned the story a third time.

"I've got to talk to Russell." Mike picked his cell phone up off the table.

"You can't call him now. It's after eleven."

"I don't think he'll mind."

Forty minutes later, Mike ended the call, then sat straight against the headboard. In silence.

"Well, are you going to tell me what's going on?" Melanie shook his arm.

"You heard my side of the conversation."

"But for once you weren't doing most of the talking."

"True. Come here." Mike lifted his arm and invited her in.

With a wary look on her face, Melanie pushed brunette bangs behind her left ear as she eased closer to her husband.

Mike moved slightly so he faced Melanie directly. He squeezed both of her shoulders and drilled deep into her eyes. "I can't explain what happened tonight. Why now? I don't know. But I've had a wake-up call. I need to turn my priorities right side up. I've allowed work to dominate my life, our lives, far too long. It isn't healthy for you, our marriage, our children, or me. I love you, and I'm sorry."

Melanie stared.

Feeling salty dew in his eyes, Mike hugged his wife tighter than he had in years. And then he shocked her even more.

His voice shook, but his words rang strong. "Lord, I'm sorry I put you on the back burner. I'm not sure if that's the right way to say it, but you and I both know it's true. And I'm sorry I hurt my wife and children by working too much. Please help me turn things around. I'm tired. Thank you for giving me rest. Amen."

Mike and Melanie talked until yawns smothered their words. Mike turned the alarm clock off. He fell asleep with Melanie in his arms. And rested as if he were in heaven's bed itself.

Mike woke Saturday with fatigue still tingling his muscles and bones. He knew one night wasn't going to make up for years of sleep deprivation. But he didn't let it stop him from enjoying a leisurely breakfast with Melanie before helping her with some yard work.

In the afternoon, they lay down and napped for a bit. He woke up groggy, but, once it wore off, he felt inspired to do a bit of creative brainstorming. In a short time, he had quite a list. Then he and Melanie went to Favanelle for a nice dinner and came home relaxed.

On Sunday, Mike surprised Melanie by getting ready for church before her.

During the service, Mike furiously scribbled notes through the sermon on Sabbath rest. He couldn't get over how much of the message seemed directed at his situation. Afterward, he pumped the pastor's hand and repeated, "Thank you," at least four times.

Mike and Melanie ate a quiet lunch, took a short nap, then drove to their oldest daughter's house to play with their grandson. It was the second big surprise of the day.

That evening, Mike snuggled with Melanie, until the two retired just before ten. Even with his afternoon nap, Mike fell asleep quickly and woke the next morning feeling fresher than he had in years.

They flirted like schoolkids over breakfast, and Mike desperately wanted to call off work. But, though he felt better, Mike remembered how strange his body felt on Friday. He pulled himself from Melanie's embrace. "I'll be home before six. Promise."

She smiled past pouty lips. "I'm counting on it."

He laughed and waved, walking out the door. But he turned and poked his head around the jamb. "I love you."

Her giggle echoed in his mind.

At the office, Mike called his doctor and made an appointment for eleven, leaving him just enough time to make the necessary changes. He pulled out Saturday's list.

One by one, Mike called men and women into his office. He interviewed them as if they were new hires, but he had specific criteria in mind. Mike cautiously rooted for signs of each candidate's integrity.

When he was done, he prayed for wisdom over the names. Then he carefully selected a group of women and men he believed to portray strong moral values and honesty, with the ability to guide others in the way of trustworthy actions.

By nine thirty, he sat in front of his chosen team and shared the new vision, along with the role each of them would fill. Major change was in the air at Myriad Marketing. When he finished delegating and was once again alone in the room, he relished the sense of new found freedom. There was still plenty of work to do, but Mike no longer felt alone. Now, there was one more thing to face.

The doctor's visit didn't turn out as well as Mike hoped. He was sent immediately to the hospital for tests, where the physicians discovered a brain clot, making him a target for an instantaneous stroke. He was immediately admitted and given strong clot-busting medicines.

Melanie was horrified at the news and stayed by his side until his release.

Three days later, the physician signed off on the paperwork. "That clot was ready to burst at any moment. It's a good thing you got here when you did."

"Thanks, Doc."

"I'm glad to see one go home healthy. But you're not out of the woods yet—make sure you follow up."

"I don't plan to keep making the same mistakes in my future." He smiled at Melanie. "It took a while, but I finally learned my lesson."

———

Mike changed his lifestyle when he discovered God's way pointed to a more satisfying life. One that allowed him to live longer. We would all do well to remember God's design is planned for our good.

Taking a full day of rest doesn't make us weaker; it makes us stronger. Allowing others to share our burdens doesn't mean we're less valuable; it proves we're needed. Asking for help doesn't mean we're less intelligent; it means we're smart enough to fill the gaps.

By admitting our needs in submission to God, he is made strong in our lives. This is one of the secrets to becoming irreplaceable.

In the final chapter, we'll make the final jump to getting hired first and fired last. Don't miss your chance to leave a mark on the world. Can you be replaced? You have a choice in the answer to that question.

—————— Investigative Questions ——————

1. Do you take a daily dose of the good medicine of laughter? (Prov. 17:22).

2. Do you allow your soul to return to rest, knowing the Lord has been good to you? (Ps. 116:7).

3. Do you keep God's Sabbaths holy, so they are a sign between you, showing you know that he is the LORD your God? (Ezek. 20:20).

Chapter 12

The Jesus Jump

Money should serve God and people—God and people are not meant to serve money.

Recently, I watched a television interview with a man who for decades lived decadently in fame and wealth as a highly successful actor. While growing up, his shows made me laugh, made me breathless, and whisked me into worlds previously unknown.

He made millions off of movies, spinoffs, and promotional products, including a doll molded in his likeness. And yet today he is destitute.

His losses extend much further than his income, financial investments, and residuals. He is relationally bankrupt. When he dies, he believes he will be alone. All who held out their hands will not extend theirs to hold his as he passes from this life. Most likely, he will be found in the tiny shack he inhabits, several days after his death.

From his own description, at the peak of his fame, this man treated others with a narcissistic approach. He gave based on his expectation of getting something in return. If he no longer needed their services, he tossed people aside. Now, he's experiencing what it feels like on the receiving end.

The opposite of what God tells us to do.

One thing that fascinates me about the Christian faith is Jesus. He doesn't use us; he gives. It isn't about what he gets out of the relationship; it's about what he can offer. Christ doesn't cram his ways down our throats. The decision is ours. Whether we believe in his authority or his word, he still loves us. Our denial doesn't change his facts.

And Jesus understands our sinful nature. The instinct of self-preservation, even if it means hurting others. But sin hurts us in the process as well—eventually.

This concept transfers into our work lives. Over the past few decades, the mantra "look out for number one" has invaded society and our subconscious thoughts. We don't realize how much it influences our attitudes—and then our actions.

In a job interview and after we are hired.

Humility and a teachable spirit are sought-after qualities. They make us irreplaceable.

I'm not trying to cram these principles down your throat. No one can make you do anything. But I can tell you from years of experience, a blasé way of thinking can destroy you. At its worst, a misdirected attitude might cost you your home, possessions, friends, and family after you've lost your job.

The wisdom in the Bible has stood the test of time, and those who follow it succeed long-term. Shortcutting might feed immediate gratification, but the illusion of success doesn't last. Those who steadily persevere, who choose character over cheating, who work with integrity, doing the same thing whether someone can see or not, win the race to happiness.

There's no greater peace than a clear conscience. And there's no faster road to transforming yourself from expendable to irreplaceable.

Becoming irreplaceable means we follow good examples. We become like those we spend time and space with. We become irreplaceable when we lead others by good habits established through determination and discipline. But arriving at a leadership position doesn't mean you can rest on your past achievements. It also doesn't mean you can use others to keep you there.

We all answer to someone. Employees answer to managers, managers answer to presidents, presidents answer to boards, boards answer to consumers. And we all answer to God. A humble offer of our services based on our abilities not only helps us but allows us to make a difference by adding positive traits to the world around us.

Families, nations, and global economies benefit from our decision to work God's way.

The joy of living for God and others allows us the lasting honor of being part of something bigger than ourselves and makes us irreplaceable. The world—and our workplaces—are better because we exist.

Irreplaceable work habits give us a deep satisfaction and inner contentment. Nothing and no one can snatch it away.

But not everyone experiences the stability of a life free from anxiety and fear of loss. Many cling to the illusion that present-day gratification will last, hoping they don't lose everything they've worked so hard for. They live in a world of fear, where paychecks are gobbled up by bills, momentary pleasures, and the worries of this world. Where companies crumble. Jack is such a person.

Comfortable in false security, while his thriving music career soared, Jack had it all, for a while. Over time, his pride took its toll on the business. When things fell apart, Jack wasn't the only one who paid for his arrogance. Others fell prey to his narcissistic decisions.

A string of employees stumbled and grumbled from the shiny silver tour bus. Like snapping dogs, they jostled positions as their words bit through the early morning air.

"Where are we?"

"Idaho. I think."

"I need coffee."

"Hurry up."

"I'm trying."

"My back hurts."

"What are you complaining about? At least you got a few hours of sleep. We didn't finish packing up the equipment until almost two."

"What's wrong with the bus?"

The group huddled on the edge of the road and stared at the plume of white steam hissing toward the dawn-streaked sky.

A pneumatic sound caused all sets of eyes to turn in unison.

Jack, the tour manager for Liberty Valiant, country music's hottest duo, breezed off the deck of his mobile mansion. He breathed deep of the mountain perfumes and rubbed his knuckles against closed eyelids. His nose wrinkled as he sipped past the bursting bubbles in his first cup of Dr Pepper.

Jack scanned a panoramic circle to evaluate the situation. He noted the slumped shoulders in the crew. A twinkling sparkle lit his gray eyes, and he forced a cheery lilt to energize his greeting. "Good morning, looks like we get an unexpected break."

"Fantastic." Devin regretted the sarcastic word before the last syllable left his mouth. He knew he was in trouble.

Jack leveled an angry glare at Devin. "Don't start."

"Sorry, Chief." After six years, Devin knew better than to argue, even though his body ached from the tornadic pace of a three-night event.

"Buck up, we've only got two more months on this tour. Then you can take all the time off you want."

"Sure, Boss." Devin had heard the empty promises before.

Jack walked away and marched toward the source of their unscheduled interruption. He stopped at the snub nose where steam continued to funnel toward low-lying clouds. The driver was on the phone, but Jack didn't wait for the other conversation to end. "What's the problem?"

"I'll get back to you." The driver ended his call. "Looks like we'll need a replacement. Boise's less than two hours."

"Get it done," Jack called over his shoulder, on the move to contend with the next situation.

The images on the side of the bus of Ted Liberty and Johnny Valiant grinned at Jack as he boarded Ted's posh home away from home. The disheveled performer padded from the bathroom. "We there?"

"Stage bus is down. Got another coming in from Boise."

"How long before I can roll?"

"Let me get the guys started on the gear. I'll talk to Johnny, and you should be good to go shortly. I've got it under control; you can go back to bed."

"I'm awake now. Think I'll grab my bike and go for a ride while I wait."

"Just don't go far, okay?" Jack respected the star's commitment to exercise, but now wasn't the time for mountain biking.

"Sure." Ted was already slipping his Under Armour over his head.

Jack watched him pedal out of sight before he peeked in on Johnny, who slept undisturbed. Now he could focus on the task at hand. He felt for his cell phone as he walked, but skipped a breath when the familiar device wasn't in his pocket.

Where did I leave it? I don't have time for this.

Once again, Jack walked up to the stage hands. "Devin, you, Tommy, and Brad open up the bins, and start yanking gear. Hurry but be careful and keep it organized. Most of the heavy stuff's on the semi, so it shouldn't take long. When that other bus gets here I want things staged so we can transition smoothly."

"Got it."

"Nathan, clean out the cabinets and then the fridge. Adam, you've got the bathroom."

Adam groaned.

"Problem?" Jack shouted expletives at the young man while he showered gravel toward him with the tip of his shoe.

Adam hustled toward the open bus door so he could avoid further attack.

"Whatever your name is," Jack nodded at Jonathan, the new kid, "grab the bedding. The rest of you boys make sure your personal belongings are ready to stow. Chop, chop, let's get to it."

Employees scattered like a pack of coyotes at the sound of gun blast. Jonathan, freshly hired and only on his sixth day, was the only one who didn't move.

"Something on your mind?" Jack demanded.

"Where do you want me to put the pillows and blankets once they're off the bus? On the ground?"

Jack slapped his forehead. "Now that makes sense, doesn't it? Am I the only one who uses their brain in this outfit? If it wasn't for me, things would fall apart. Fold them neatly, then stack them on top of the luggage. Now move it. You're costing me money."

Jonathan's face turned red as he rushed to get away.

In a short time, with his first batch of bedding overflowing out of his arms, Jonathan waddled back off the bus. Other than a couple of guitar cases, and a drum, there was nothing on the ground. No personal bags.

Jonathan whispered to Devin, "What do I do now? There's no luggage to put this stuff on."

Devin pulled a couple of pillows from under Jonathan's chin and placed them on the drum. "First, we need to fold those blankets better." He nodded at the balled-up pile in Jonathan's hands. "Jack's a real neat-freak."

Jonathan expelled a long breath. "Thanks. I don't think he likes me."

Devin walked his half of the red fleece blanket toward Jonathan. They met in the middle. "Don't take it personal. He gets himself all worked up. Burns fast and hot. Then half the time, later, he can't remember what he was mad about."

Jonathan smoothed their melded corners and placed the red blanket squarely on one of the black amplifiers Tommy deposited from the bin under the bus.

Devin had just picked up a blue quilt, when he glanced toward the front of the bus. He shoved the cottony mass at Jonathan's chest and immediately took strides away. "Put your head down, here comes Jack."

Jonathan snatched the unfolded bedding and scurried onto the bus where he could work out of sight.

Jack reached Devin as he hoisted a brown Docker's suitcase onto the roadside. "Did you find my cell?"

"Is it missing?"

"I told you to look for it."

"You didn't say anything about your phone. You just told me to unload this gear." Devin patted the duffle bag in his hands.

"Don't argue with me, I told you to find my phone first, then unload. How do you think I'm going to let anyone know we'll be late?"

Knowing Jack had either thought the directive and not spoken out loud or told someone else and in his faulty memory mistaken that person for him, Devin let the brunt of Jack's fury pass. "Sorry. I'll get right on it. Where's the last place you saw it?"

Jack scuffed his right foot over a few pebbles and avoided eye contact. "I had it when I woke up. I don't know if I left it in Ted's bus, Johnny's, in mine or if I dropped it somewhere between stops."

"Don't worry, I'll find it."

"Let me know when you do." Without offering the slightest look of gratitude, Jack hurried off to find his next victim.

Jack's phone was perched beside the vented hood on the broken-down bus. Jack said nothing when Devin offered it in his outstretched hand.

He simply seized it and commenced dialing. Jack's wife was the unfortunate recipient.

"I need you to call the promoter."

"Good morning and I love you too."

"Don't get smart."

"Yes, sir. And just what am I supposed to tell them?"

"Tell them one of our buses broke down but a replacement's on the way. We'll be a couple of hours late. Make sure sound and lighting has everything ready; Johnny and Ted will start checks as soon as we arrive."

"Are you okay?"

"I don't have time for small talk." Jack imagined a black funnel, his hundred dollar bills whisked into someone else's pockets. "You know lost time means lost money."

"Excuse me for worrying."

"There's nothing to worry about. Now will you take care of it?"

"I'm not one of your hired men."

"Don't get melodramatic."

"Whatever you say, Master." Terry hung up.

Jack wallowed in self-pity. No one ever noticed how hard he worked to make things run smoothly. It made him push the boys even harder.

He even yelled at Ted when the artist showed up ten minutes after the equipment transfer to the new bus was complete. Jack was ready to go.

The look on Ted's face flashed a warning, although nothing was said in the moment.

They made the concert venue with plenty of time to spare, and everyone calmed down. Everyone, that is, except Jack.

As the tour progressed, Jack's mood escalated in greater degrees of rage. He spewed long tirades at production staff, band members, and road crews. He unleashed wrathful tongue lashings if they didn't understand his disjointed instructions. Several new hires quit without notice under Jack's barrage of powerful profanities.

Some employees stayed and impersonated Jack's management style. Looking like their leader, they verbally kicked those with less authority and often blindsided the next person to cross their path. The dominoes fell along the tour path for Liberty Valiant.

The atmosphere around Jack was charged with negativity and confusion. He stormed one minute and then, without warning, attempted to charm those he'd hurt with flattering words and unintentioned promises.

Jack even threw God's name around. Periodically he'd say, "I'm a blessed man and I know it. God sure does take care of me." He secretly hoped that public acknowledgment would keep the financial gifts pouring in.

For a while, Jack seemed to flourish in spite of his rants. But the mishmash of moods created a culture of unrest around him.

Never knowing which Jack they'd get kept employees on edge. And the more Jack raged at people publicly, the more his employees acted out in rebellion.

More and more, his habit of disrespect spilled onto promoters, label execs, and other managers. His ulterior motives wouldn't stay tucked behind the mask he attempted to wear.

When consequences caught up with him, Jack tried to turn things around. But it was too late.

In less than three years, he was forced out of his job. Jack's methods burned many bridges for Liberty Váliant, and their popularity suffered as a result. He lost his power and his profit sharing.

Jack went on to work with a few other top performers, but the pattern was set. His sick mix of arrogance and desperation caused his worst fears to come true. He'd lose another position, though he clutched until the very end. No one could stand to be around him.

When Jack died, the former millionaire was destitute, in more ways than one. Terry divorced him years before. His children didn't speak to him. Jack's remaining relationships all ended in bitter estrangements. People he'd thought were friends disappeared when the money ran dry.

Jack used up everyone in his efforts to rescue his profits. But he labored in vain. Money, the true god in Jack's life, deserted him in the last years of his life. His god didn't hold his hand when he died.

Today, success too often is measured in dollars and power. But we forget how elusive those things are. Like vaporous images, they flit in and out of our lives.

True success is measured in living with meaningful purpose. It gives us a reason to get out of bed in the morning and is better than any energy drink.

Successful people help others, act in humility, make intentional decisions for the greater good, take courage, and dare to be different. The reward is a sense of inner well-being that no amount of money can buy.

Echo the habits of those exampled in this book and in the Bible. Set yourself apart from the crowd clamoring for successful work. Investigate yourself and see whether you're choosing irreplaceable behaviors. Ask these questions:

- Do you dare to be different like Joseph?
- Are you a great follower like Ruth?
- Like David, do you discipline yourself to take responsibility?
- Do your words matter like Jacob's?
- Are your patterns effective like Paul's?
- Like Esther, do you take courage for such a time as this?
- Do you pay back more than you take like Zacchaeus?
- Are you measuring your position like Matthew?
- Like Moses, do your problems promise the power of miracles?
- Do you take decisive action like Deborah?
- Are you resting to improve productivity like Jethro?
- Like Jesus, have you jumped into irreplaceable actions?

When you read the life of Jesus in the New Testament of the Bible, you find he exemplifies all of these traits in the work he was called to do. Before he taught, he lived the principles set forth by God prior to earth's creation. His personal life was in order.

Get your personal life in order to make yourself a better employee. I believe you can conduct your life in such a way that you are the first one hired and last one fired. Even in the most challenging economic climates, your value will shine out in the crowd.

And remember that leaders are not immune to the ravages of tough job markets. Often, they are the first let go when money gets tight in a company. Trimming the fat only makes sense. Owners who manage ineffectively can stand alone in a dying consumer market.

So how can leaders protect themselves, and the employees who trust them, when desperate times call for desperate measures? One thing's certain: operating out of panic does not work. And trying to hide your fear under selfish choices will do nothing but place your job on the chopping block.

However, it's never too late for a fresh start with fresh faith. Jack's pride and panic were safely ensconced below his arrogant demands. His narcissistic treatment of others was a poor mask for the insecurities rolling under his thin skin. But watch what happens when he makes the jump to Jesus' example.

—⁘—

The crimson bleed of an early morning sunrise lit the darkness under Jack's eyelids. Rocking air brakes caused him to blink awake.

He stumbled out of bed, threw on jeans and a polo shirt, then poured a bubbling Dr Pepper into a cup of ice, his caffeine of choice, and padded down the steps of his tour bus.

Jack acknowledged the crew huddled outside the gurgling silver coach ahead of his. He walked past, giving them space to vent, while he visited the driver of the steaming bus. Jack listened to the man's assessment—they needed to switch vehicles. It would take a while for the new bus to arrive from Boise.

Jack walked back and spoke to the disgruntled pack of men. "I realize this isn't the kind of break we're looking for and it's frustrating, but let's give it twenty minutes and regroup. I need to review something, and then we'll talk.

He hurried up the steps he'd dismounted a few minutes earlier. Jack cracked open the worn Bible and placed it on his lap. His morning chapter, in the book of Luke, offered sage wisdom directly from the words of Christ. Fitting for the occasion.

When Jack finished and carefully closed the hardbound book, he lingered to caress its cover in reflective thought. Then he slid to the floor and scooted on his knees, close to the couch cushion where he'd just sat.

He intertwined his fingers, closed his eyes, and bowed his head. "Lord, help me imitate Jesus in my role as leader today. Thank you for making me a shrewd manager as well as a gentle and compassionate leader. I praise you for giving me the gift of discernment, the courage to act upon my abilities, and the wisdom to know when to keep silent. Let there be more of you and less of me. Amen."

Next, Jack went to check on Ted and Johnny. With each step, he prayed a blessing over every man he worked with by name. He made sure to include thanks for them as people, not simply employees.

Johnny was sleeping, and Ted took off on a bike ride, leaving Jack free to initiate the details for their bus transfer.

"How's everyone this fine Monday morning?" he greeted the circle of men.

Devin spouted, "Tired."

Trying not to let Devin's negative energy draw him down, Jack offered a sympathetic grimace. "I know. You guys worked hard this weekend, and I really appreciate your efforts. I'm sure the fans did, too." Jack patted Devin's shoulder. "Let's talk about what needs to be done. The sooner we get started, the sooner we'll be on our way. Devin, why don't you tell us what you think we need to tackle first."

Devin straightened a bit taller, and a few other shoulders perked up as well. The group of twelve talked through the entire transfer process in less than five minutes. Most of them had at least two years' experience on the job, so unforeseen problems didn't throw them.

When something fell apart, the group teamworked a plan to fix the broken process, instead of blaming individuals. They'd experienced more than one miracle along the way.

Devin took Jonathan, the new guy, under his wing and mentored him along. In the manner Jack had taught him.

They were ready for the second bus long before it arrived. And even then, Ted didn't get back until ten minutes after. Jack took a deep breath and prayed, "Father, forgive him for he doesn't know it causes others frustration." He hoped it was all right to chuckle at his own twist on a familiar prayer.

Things weren't perfect, but the atmosphere on the tour was much calmer than in the years prior to Jack's study of the Bible. He was taking more time with his family and putting less pressure on others.

A few months later, Jack was offered a similar job working for a well-known Christian artist. In the interview, one particular question gave Jack pause.

"Is there anything unconfessed and unrepented that might keep God from blessing our work together?"

Instantly, a momentary panic washed over Jack's heart. "That's a tough one. I really want this job, but I need time to honestly evaluate my answer before telling you what I think you want to hear."

"Call when you're ready."

Back home with Terry, he talked to his wife about the magnitude of the question he needed to answer. "In years past, I had things backwards. I used God and people to serve money, instead of the other way around. Until today, I didn't realize I hadn't confessed it out loud."

"God knows you're sorry," Terry comforted.

"But I'm supposed to go to those I hurt and ask forgiveness. You are at the top of the list. Will you forgive me for thinking only of myself?"

Terry's lower lids puffed with fat balls of water. "Yes." Her voice raspy, she added, "Thank you."

As the door to confession opened for the first time in their home, Jack and Terry covered areas never discussed before. An ambience of deep healing blanketed their relationship, and they knew it was more than a feeling. It would last.

Just before nodding off to sleep, Jack bent and kissed the tip of Terry's nose. "When I married you, I got the whole package."

Jack spent a few days making calls, writing e-mails, and sending texts. He took more than one former employee to lunch for a private meal so he could listen and learn about how his mistakes had hurt someone else. He was becoming a new person, and he wanted God's blessing on this next chapter of his life.

It was more than a week before Jack called with a clear conscience to answer the difficult question. "To my knowledge, there is nothing unconfessed that would keep God from blessing our work together."

He was offered the job and gladly accepted.

As the tour manager for a famous artist, Jack faced periodic episodes of narcissism, in others and himself. A Christian atmosphere didn't make challenges disappear. In times of pressure, human insecurity rattled everyone.

But Jack decided to fight back through the words and life of Jesus, to step up with renewed determination, and to trust his faith more than his fears. It carried him, and those who followed his example, through many challenges.

Jack thrived by encouraging others and reached out to those who continued to struggle. His steady focus on serving God and people pushed many to hang on when they felt like giving up.

His last decades of work extended beyond music, and over time he was asked to help an international ministry. He invested his talents in caring for orphans and widows when catastrophic events took fathers and husbands.

On the day Jack passed from life on earth to life in paradise, lines of people streamed to comfort his family. They waited hours to hug Terry. A blur of mourners shared their personal stories about Jack's genuine kindness and eased the sting of death for his children and grandchildren.

The preacher summed his life with this statement: "Jack worked God's way, making more of others and less of himself. He'll reap the rewards of those choices for eternity. The world is a better place because he existed. No one will ever replace Jack."

What will people say about you when you leave this earth?

At the end of this book, I can't tell you how to live your life or how to work. Just as God doesn't shove himself down the throats of people he loves and desires to help, I don't want to shove unwanted information at you. So I'll simply end with a few questions.

What if you followed some of the examples in this book and none of them made a difference? Would you be any worse off than you are right now?

But—what if changing nothing made matters worse? What if you had the power to practice different habits and improve your value at work, at home, and in the world at large?

What if there's power in the ancient text of the Bible and you miss it? What if your whole life passes and you fail to live up to your potential and reap the rewards of deep satisfaction?

What if you miss career opportunities and allow another to become irreplaceable in your stead? Imagine, however, answers to a different set of questions:

- What if you practiced the millennial wisdom found in the Bible and started making a difference at your workplace?
- What if you followed the example of characters who show us what integrity looks like?
- What if God began to bless the work of your hands?
- What if your territory expanded and you started impacting the area in which you live?

- What if, like the men and women we researched, your influence moved outward and you changed your nation?
- What if your resolve to change changed the world?
- What if your efforts saved the livelihoods and lives of many people?
- What if you could become irreplaceable but let the opportunity pass?

Do not fear answering that special call on your life to do the work prepared for you before you were born. I believe if we are to succumb to a fear, it should be this. Fear missing out on the adventure that awaits, more than you fear what you can't see.

Maybe it's doing things differently right where you are, or maybe it's exploring new territories. Ask God—then listen. There you will find the answer.

My final challenge is this—try the principles outlined in this book for three months. Answer the investigative questions at the end of each chapter honestly. Go to my website, www.brooksanita.com, and review the Five Regrets of the Dying. Then study the Five Fresh Starts for the Living.

If this investment doesn't produce a positive difference, what has it hurt?

Three months? I challenge you to take action. If this is the worst thing you try, you've had a really great life.

Money won't fix your problems. It won't hold your hand when you die. Honoring God and helping others with the work of your hands will ensure you leave an irreplaceable legacy.

At the beginning of this book, I asked, "Can anyone be replaced?" In my estimation, based on several years of experience, both as an employee and a leader, I believe you can make yourself irreplaceable in any job market. But it takes practice.

You were designed with abilities, talents, and promise. Invest wisely, work diligently, and share generously. Allow your commitment to ripple onto people, communities, nations, and our world. Make a difference where you are.

With determination, in the face of an unknown future, you can become irreplaceable. The first hired and last fired. Say yes to the adventure, and come share in your Master's happiness.

————— Investigative Questions —————

1. On this day, which do you choose for yourself, blessings or curses? (Deut. 28).

2. Do you rob God and yourself? (Mal. 3:8–10).

3. Are you attempting to gain the whole world, only to forfeit your soul? (Mark 8:36).

Notes

[1] "Work Related Stress—What about Stress at Home?" *Health and Safety Executive*, http://www.hse.gov.uk/stress/furtheradvice/stressathome.htm, accessed June 2012.

[2] The Marlin Company, "Economy Up, Worker Stress Down? Think Again. Results from the Marlin Company Workplace Survey," www.themarlincompany.com, June 15, 2010.

[3] Timothy Pychyl, "Procrastination: Oops, Where Did the Day Go?" *Psychology Today*, September 6, 2011, http://www.psychologytoday.com/articles/201109/procrastination-oops-where-did-the-day-go, accessed July, 2012.

[4] Alcee L. Hastings, "Human Trafficking in the United States," http://www.alceehastings.house.gov/index.php?option=com_content&view=article&id=665:human-trafficking-in-the-united-states&catid=60, accessed September, 2012.